C000124769

HOUSE SHARE HERO

What all Landlords should know about:

HMOs, HiMOs, Houses in Multiple Occupancy, Letting Rooms, Renting Rooms, Rooms to Rent, and Rooms to Let.

by

Steve Julien

First published by Hometime UK Ltd in the United
Kingdom 2009. Updated in 2011.
Housesharehero.co.uk

Copyright 2009 and 2011 © Steve Julien

None of the contents of this book can be copied or
publicly used without permission from the author.

Copy-writer and Editor: Bernadette Morris
Cover design and Artwork: Linda Koperski

Acknowledgements

Along with all my property and business friends and mentors, I would especially like to thank all friends and family members who have contributed to the creation of *House Share Hero*.
Namely: My wonderful wife, Suzie, for being my rock; Mum, Dad and Don for their love; Julie Shaw, Jez Pang and Ian Johnston for putting up with me in the early days; Neil Mather, Angela Rosella, for giving me a chance; Jenny Poole for giving me a push; Bernie for being the literal 'Ying' to my illiteral 'Yang', and Linda for her amazing artwork.

I would also like to thank Rachael Dudley and Arthur Kemp for making all the numbers work so beautifully, and finally the (mostly) amazing people I'm lucky enough to have renting from me!

Contents

Dedications

To
Suzie, Mya, Theo, Mum, Dad, Don, Christine and Malcolm.

Foreword

It's about time... We use this phrase so often without really understanding its implication: that this thing called 'time' is beyond our control. In fact, it controls most people for the best part of their lives.

And it seems quite ironic that even in this age of high technology, labour and time-saving devices and with a super, worldwide, electronic communication system, we still find ourselves with no time to actually live our lives, or do anything that we really want to do. This is because the more time we have, the more we are expected to give up to the endless business of working.

The following story is about one man who gained mastery of time, and not only beat it into submission, but made it work *for* him instead of against, so that he is now in complete control of his own time and therefore his life.

This is a fascinating insight into the building of an empire by someone who has been through the rat-race and won with flying colours.
It really is about time someone did.

Bernie Morris

INTRODUCTION

Owning and managing house shares has given me time.

More time than I ever had when I was a slave to the J.O.B. I don't have a crystal ball, but I plan for it to give me even more valued time in the future.

I'm still in my thirties and want to make the absolute most of the fifty, sixty or seventy+ years I have left!

When I started buying property, I thought money was my carrot. Since then, I have realised it isn't; it's just the shiny green vehicle that chauffeurs me to more time every day along with a richer, happier and more fulfilled life.

Before I had my own time and, only a few years ago, a typical day would go like this:

Woken up at 7am by the alarm clock, I wait a moment for it to kick in. Then it does. The bottle of Shiraz I drank last night, to get over the boredom and stress of the day before, is now taking its toll. Luckily, I had a bottle the night before that and also the night before that, so it feels no different to any other weekday morning. Plus, I am expecting it, so have already screwed up my face in anticipation.

I turn the alarm clock off, vow to get up in five minutes and next thing I know its 7:45am. Bugger.

My hangover is worse than first anticipated. I forgot about the pint or two I had after work with a colleague, as a starter to my bottle of wine when I got home. We each looked and felt like an embodiment of the line from the Paul Simon song: *You can call me Al.*

Why were we 'so **soft** in the middle' when 'the rest of our lives were so **hard**'?

Lying there in bed, I decide, like I do every morning, to have just one glass of wine tonight.

The shower helps, but I've barely got time to get dry before squeezing into the shiny suit the bank has supplied, which seems to be getting smaller by the week, unlike the dark circles around my eyes.

I can't afford a car, so start walking the thirty-minute journey to work. It looks like rain when I leave the house, which is soon confirmed and I haven't got an umbrella. There are only terraced houses within half a mile of where I live and lazy people with poorly trained dogs make this local walk a bit of a nightmare. If there's ever a 'dog poo lottery' then I'm living it!

By the time I get to work I'm starving. My suit has repelled a lot of the water but I'm left with a soggy 'V' on my chest.

I arrive late for the morning sales meeting and, along with five other lethargic sales managers, pledge allegiance to various mantras of 'thinking outside the bar', 'raising the envelope' and 'pushing the imaginary box' – or some equally overused corporate nonsense.

The branch manager pulls me to one side and asks me why I haven't shaved; I lie and tell him I'm growing a beard.

After the meeting, I go and sit on the toilet until they bang on the door to tell me my first appointment's here. Oh joy!

I spend the morning selling people products I don't believe in, or am sure they don't really need, whilst in between munching on a cashier's sandwiches that I've found in the fridge. It's a double win for him as they taste awful and I've agreed to buy him a burger for lunch.

I spend most of the afternoon hiding on the stairs that lead to the fire escape and subsequently don't hit the unreachable target set by my manager.

The area manager collars me at 4:57.pm on my way out of the door and wonders why I'm not staying late to call customers and make sales appointments, seeing as I haven't got any booked in for the rest of the week. He lectures me in a patronising way about the importance of commitment and reminds me that a winner never quits and a quitter never wins.

Outside, I kick myself for not having the backbone to tell him to stick his job where the sun doesn't shine. On the way home I get even wetter and tread in more dog poo which somehow manages to find its way into one of my turn-ups.

I arrive home at 5:47, head straight for a bottle of wine and cook dinner, relieved that another day is over and that there's only Thursday and Friday to get through.

I burn my dinner and remember that I'm also working Saturday this week...

Nowadays, if I choose to work, my days go more like this:

Woken up between 5:30-6:30am on a weekday! Not really the time I wish to wake up, but that's when Junior does and he's just a baby.

"Its too early, son" is a term he has yet to understand. I've made my bed and it's a shame I can't lie-in in it!

I feel tired but relaxed and can now hear my three-year-old daughter in her room singing in an operatic voice:

"Gordon Pear" (Go compare)

She hasn't a clue what an insurance comparison website is, but likes the man on the advert.

It's my turn to get up with her, so we go downstairs and I make a coffee. We chill out for an hour and they play while I lie on the floor like a semi-conscious climbing frame.

The coffee kicks in and we pick a music channel and have a dance.

My wife comes down an hour later and I jump in the shower for half an hour or so.

As I listen to the local radio station and brush my teeth, the 'Eye in the Sky' reports several traffic jams, an accident and some road closures due to works. I'm alone, so can smile about it without looking too smug.

I get dressed, grab a bowl of cereal and some juice, open the front door and make the seven-second commute to my office.

There's a nip in the air but the under-floor heating in the garage I've had converted to an office, means I'm soon feeling 'toasty'.

I switch the computer on and munch away while it's firing up.

I have nearly 100 rental units and, checking my emails, I see that a couple of things have happened overnight.

1. Michelle has left her keys at work again. At 11pm she got off the late bus and can't get into the house. She has called my 24-hour help line, which connects her to a generic call centre about 150 miles away. Their software identifies the number she has called as mine and a message flashes up on the screen telling the operator to smile and say "Hello Hometime UK, xxxx speaking, how can I help?". Once Michelle has explained her predicament, she is put on hold while the operator looks at my company file notes for instructions. She finds a number for my general maintenance guy who she calls and he says he will be there in twenty minutes. The operator thanks Michelle for calling my company and tells her that the locksmith will be there in less than half an hour. Michelle is happy when he arrives after twenty minutes to let her in with a master key and is pleased that he has only charged her £40 instead of the normal £50.

2. At 1am, Phil, who has moved into a brand new property, which I have just completed on the day before, decides to christen the bath only to find out that the plumber who installed it hadn't connected the waste pipe properly and, when he pulls the plug out, the kitchen starts to flood. He hasn't worked out why the kitchen is flooding, has lost my

24-hour help line number so calls my mobile. When not turned on, my mobile is diverted to my call centre; the operator tells him not to worry and he will send out an emergency plumber within the hour. My plumber arrives bleary-eyed within half an hour and fixes the problem. Phil is happy and I forward the hefty invoice my plumber has already emailed me onto the house builder to pay.

3. One of my long term sharers has bought a house so has moved out. His replacement has moved in later that evening and, although none of her housemates (or me) were there when she arrived and the house and room are securely locked, she has had no trouble getting in and is pleased that her room is spotlessly clean, the pc desk she requested has already been installed and a copy of her tenancy agreement is waiting for her. When her housemates do get back, they greet her by name, show her where everything is and make her a cup of tea.

All in all, a busy few hours since I last checked in, but everything has been handled without my direct intervention.

There have also been several calls from people looking for places to live. I have their full details as they have spoken to a real person and not been asked to leave a message. However, my houses are all full with nothing coming up for six to eight weeks. I forward these to other landlords who I know have empty units, as most in turn will do the same for me when I need good people and they are full.

Their details are also inputted into a very simple piece of free software, so that on exactly the same time every Sunday evening (a time that most people are likely to fancy a change of job, partner and most importantly for me, house share!) they receive a personal notification from me about the 'great places' we have coming up that they have told me they would like. This is sent to them for as long as they are happy to receive it or until they rent from me, whichever comes first. The notification is up to date but was compiled days or even weeks before, takes less than two minutes for me to arrange and reaches thousands of people.

Once they are renting from me, the contact from me is still personal and regular, but the emphasis is now on retention through great service along with some occasional and gentle 'upselling'.

I update my mp3 player, adding some more tracks, and head off to the gym. It's 11am so just a couple of pensioners and mums to negotiate on the roads, which entertains me greatly as my new sports coupe has a monster V6 engine, stiff chassis and brain quicker than mine to keep me out of trouble.

I have a good work out, another long shower and, after lunch with another landlord, I meet the family and we go to a local park to feed the ducks.

There are three or four calls to take during the afternoon. A couple of questions from suppliers and a job or two to delegate, but nothing too difficult and we all get home about 4.pm.

As my properties are full, I keep my phone on but switch it to divert. My call centre will text as well as email any messages, so if anything does come through I can choose to deal with it then and there, or leave it until tomorrow.

Just after 4pm, I check my emails and switch everything off until the morning, leaving only my personal mobile on, which the call centre have if the crap really does hit the fan which rarely happens.

I still have busy days, but when I do, I'm generally done by 2 or 3pm with maybe an occasional appointment for early evening viewings a couple of times a month, but I love what I do, so I don't mind.

In the past though, and when I used to do things the hard way, sometimes things could go wrong, very, very wrong...

CHAPTER ONE

WHEN HOUSE MATES ATTACK

I stood in the hallway and shook hands with Jack; he seemed like a nice guy.

He'd moved into one of my house shares that morning and had been referred from another good sharer of mine. This is a great way for me to find the best sharers as, generally, people will hang out or work with 'people like them' and I'm always amazed when I ask other landlords and find they're not efficiently tapping into this source.

It was the first time I'd met him in person and we were both pleased that he was in one of my properties. I was, because I'd had a vacancy to fill and he, because he hadn't seen the place before moving in and had been relying on his friend's description, along with a few photos.

I had interviewed him extensively over the phone and he'd passed with flying colours. I thought highly of the guy who'd put him in touch with me so had been happy to arrange things without meeting beforehand.

This was something that happened very rarely but it looked like I had made a good choice.

I'd particularly wanted to meet him today for two reasons.

1. Just to have a general chat and confirm my initial feelings about him. I also knew that he would be relaxed after moving in, so any verbal 'slip ups' he might make would be more likely to happen under my casual interrogation – I mean conversation.

2. As his office was closing and merging with one locally and he was the first to arrive, I wanted to be sure that I was everyone who was relocating first choice for a great place to live and that he felt enough incentive to do the bulk of the work in getting them to me. Who?

It was a bright sunny day and, as we were chatting, I suddenly became hot; then very hot... Then a mini furnace fired up just below my ribcage.

I hadn't heard what Jack had just said to me but had a general gist of the conversation so carried on nodding.

He was still smiling but I could see a growing look of concern in his eyes. Neither of us spoke about this concern but we both knew it was there. He was telling me about his train journey, but by this time I wasn't making any effort to follow the conversation.

I noticed him taking a step back as I exhaled sharply and my forehead corrugated. He was looking at me in the same way 'McGee' did every week at the start of *The Incredible Hulk* after wishing he hadn't poked mild-mannered little David Banner with a psychological stick and made him angry.

I was now leaning forward with one hand on the fifth stair, the other holding my stomach and my back arching. Man, was I in pain.

The pain lessened after a few moments and I was now able to sit on the step. My discomfort was now at an 'operational level' so I thought I had better fill Jack in on what had just happened in the half hour before we had met. It was a time when my landlord powers had been tested to breaking point by an unhinged, but surprisingly strong, six-and-a-half stone foe who we will call 'Nucking Futs', or just 'Nuts' for short.

Nuts had moved into a house share up the road about eighteen months before. It was an executive house with professional housemates and in an affluent part of the city. Nuts was only just offered a room by me and, if I'm honest, I knew there was a good chance I was letting one 'slip through the net' when I handed over the keys. She did, however, have a very good job and a sparkly reference from her previous landlord who she had lived with. It was the type of reference you would only really give to one of your kids, someone you were sleeping with, or someone who was ruining your life to the point where you would do all you could to get them out of it before they consumed your soul and turned you into a self-harming, dribbling wreck. You know, one of those 'too good to be true' types of reference.

Anyway, over the course of the time that Nuts was there, her employer gave her the boot, but her parents, back on her home world, made sure that the rent was paid like clockwork, as I imagine they preferred to love little Nuts from afar.

With time on her hands, her amusing quirks had now become disturbing obsessions. These included: washing her hands every three minutes, making sure that for every litre of water that came out of the tap, an equal amount would be splashed on the floor to drown the floor demons. She also left territory markers around the house in the form of pots, pans and other small items that no one else was allowed to touch.

Nuts insisted that no one else used the bathroom after 8.pm and advised me at least three times a week that the police were giving her protection from the 'International drug-dealing psychopath' who lived upstairs (Brian, a polite young graduate who worked for an I.T. company).

She would roam the house during the day but stay locked in her room in the evening when the others were home, sending me emails about the terrible things that the drug dealer was doing or that he had flushed a toilet at 8:03.pm. The other house mates always said Brian was as calm and laid-back as a Hindu cow and, in my experience of him, I agreed. She had also taken to writing him threatening notes and letters, predicting his downfall, which she would pin to his door or hide under his cheese in the fridge.

When anyone else was at home, the only time she left her self-imposed cell was for the twenty times per hour she would have to wash her hands.

After receiving a few gentle moans from the other house mates and my fifth email from her in as many hours – this time Brian had not only used that bathroom after 8.pm but had also left a tiny splash on the seat, causing her to short circuit – I issued her with an eviction notice.

This was my first hint that there might be trouble.

It was clear that her adaptation to our earth ways was regressing; she was unkempt, losing weight and slightly grubby (apart from her hands which I must say always looked spotless).

Although not necessary, I tried to get her to sign something to say that she had received the notice but, surprisingly, she declined, saying she was unable to do that as she wasn't well enough to hold a pen. However, she had no trouble thumping my car as hard as she could, as I was leaving.

The eviction notice gave her two months to find another place to haunt and advised that her deposit would be paid back to her by cheque once her room and the house had been inspected for damage, etc.

Not surprisingly, she said she would not accept a cheque, so was told that someone would meet her at the house to collect the keys and give back her deposit in cash. All she had to do was give us a bit of notice and make sure it was during office hours (a very flexible forty hour window).

In true Nuts fashion, she emailed at the last minute to say that 9.am on a Sunday Morning was the only time she could fit us in. Obviously her jobless, obsessive schedule was very hectic!

As I couldn't find anyone else to meet her, I bit the bullet and told her I would see her then.

At 10.am on the Sunday in question, I was sitting in the grounds of a very elegant stately home, having a coffee and a caramel slice with the family, surrounded by toffs. The only thing I don't like about toffs is their sheer toffiness and their love of wanting everyone else in the vicinity to hear about their 'high class' problems.

"The help isn't helpful enough", – "I just can't get hold of my usual supplier of 'chat pap neuf'," and "We only just got Tarquin into the private school to which his sister Tarquinetta goes. It's very over subscribed you know what with all this 'new money' about."

At 10:01.am I jumped up: "Oh crap!" I had set a reminder on my work mobile to remind me to put a reminder in my personal mobile to meet Nuts at 9.am Sunday, but had forgotten to do it! I hadn't even got my work phone on me so couldn't call her.

We left straightaway and headed for her house. I dropped my family at the nearby shopping centre and carried on to the property.

Nuts was there with all her bags packed, looking understandably hacked-off. I felt terrible as, although I was evicting her, it's important to me to provide all of my customers with good service – whatever the circumstances. I decided it was best not to show it on this occasion.

I apologised for being late and, surprisingly, Nuts didn't seem that bothered. I also noticed the lounge window was open; it's a 'tilt and turn' type which means it can be opened like a window and also like a door due to its special hinge design. I closed the window as Nuts looked on and now seemed oddly agitated by my action.

I went upstairs to check her room while she followed. My stride isn't unduly long but Nuts took about three steps to my one. I felt like Tom Cruise being followed by Dustin Hoffman in the film *Rain Man*; I half expected a smoke alarm to go off and for her to start banging herself on the side of her head, screaming.

We checked the room; it was just about acceptable. There were a few marks on the wall, a couple of stains on the mattress – one of which looked like the map of Italy – and a bit of trim missing off the wardrobe. There was also a tatty-looking cabinet in the room that she told me was mine and I couldn't really be bothered to dispute. I wasn't really thorough as I just wanted her out and was thinking of a piece of advice that a burly, prison officer, house sharer of mine had once told me.

"Never turn your back on 'em and make sure you're between them and the door."

For some reason my mind also wandered to another gem that I'd been given by an estate agent.

"Always reverse your car into spaces, just in case you have to make a quick getaway."

I hadn't done either of these.

I don't claim to have a sixth sense, but I was starting to think something was awry. I snapped out of it. Nuts was just five feet tall and I outweighed her by at least four or five stone.

I told her all was fine, collected her keys, threw them on the bed and locked the room with my master key. I use a restricted key system which means you can't copy them without a blank key from me, as high street locksmiths don't stock them and more specialist ones recognise what types of keys they are and generally won't make copies without a letter on headed paper. Of course there are always ways round this, but Nuts wasn't the type to work them out.

I started to wonder why that window had been open downstairs.

We went back down and I pulled the deposit out of my pocket, completely in cash as promised. I wasn't sure why Nuts was getting twitchier but was keeping a wary eye on her.

I asked her to take her bags outside but she told me in broken English, "Me no go now, me go later or moro."

I sighed. This could cause me a problem because she still had four weeks left on her two-month eviction notice, so technically there was nothing I could do about it. I was wondering if the fact that she had returned the keys meant she had officially relinquished her right to stay there, but I'd never come across this before so didn't know.

I thought about the half-eaten caramel slice and Americano coffee that I had left behind.

I told her that unless she removed her items from the house, she hadn't officially moved out so I wasn't going to give back her deposit until she did. I didn't offer to give her the keys back at that point but decided I would if she asked for them.

She then told me: "Me no go moro then, me go later today, deposit now pleeeaazz!"

I reminded her once again that her stuff was still in the house and she started shouting things in a language I didn't understand and lugging her stuff outside onto the street.

Normally I would have been a gentleman and helped, but in no way did I want to be seen as 'Moving her out'. Perhaps I was being over-cautious, but I wanted to make sure that there was no way this could be seen as anything other than her leaving of her own accord.

Along with her luggage, there were about five or six black bin bags full of stuff. She told me these were rubbish and I thanked her for letting me get rid of them for her. She didn't laugh.

There we stood: me on the inside doormat, her on the outside mat with her back to me, just putting her last bag on the floor. She had her left foot outside on the path and her right foot still on the inside doormat. I saw that but, stupidly, thought nothing of it.

I had my right foot on the inside doormat, with my foot and knee acting like a wedge against the back of the door, and handed her the deposit. Something wasn't right here; I was glad I'd shut the window and decided to check the back door before I went.

I placed my left hand on the door frame, creating a barrier, and I started to wish her all the best for the future, but she'd gone; one moment she was there and then, like some David Copperfieldesque illusion, I couldn't see her. What the—

Somehow – I'm still not sure how, she had run under my left arm through the tiny gap and was now scuttling through the lounge towards the kitchen. I optimistically thought she must have left something behind, and stayed for a second to watch her bags in case someone half-inched them. I then heard her say, "Me no go now, me go moro".

I sighed again and wandered slowly into the kitchen. Not only had she got her deposit, I was pretty sure I was going to have to give her the keys back as she hadn't actually left!

When I got to the kitchen she had got a frying pan, put some oil in it and was heating it up on the hob. This was odd, but then Nuts *was* odd and I was completely stumped. I told her what she had just done was wrong and asked her for the deposit back.

I wasn't surprised when she didn't even turn round but said, "No! My money!"

I asked again and got a similar answer. I was all out of ideas.

The last thing I thought of at that moment was that I might be in any danger whatsoever.

Nuts turned round; my hopes lifted as I thought she might be leaving.

I was wrong; there was now a pan full of hot oil flying towards me.

The pan hit me in the chest then fell to the floor. The oil splattered onto my clothes, left arm and left hand.
I later realised that I'd been extremely lucky on three points:

1. The frying pan hadn't actually travelled very far.
2. I was wearing a thick top over my t-shirt; silly for a warm day really, but it kept the oil off.
3. The pan had loads of oil in, so hadn't had time to get scalding hot. It was just 'hot'.

We both stood there before panic set in. I looked around the kitchen and could see large knives, other pans, bottles, a rolling pin and a frozen pork chop on the side.

Sharp and hard objects everywhere that I was determined weren't coming into contact with my soft body!

Nuts was coming towards me with a focused look on her face, her eye twitching and talking in tongues.

I threw both arms around her and got her in a bear hug, keeping my face away from hers to avoid any spitting, biting, or a head butt.

She smelled funny, but I was committed. I decided to get her as far away from me as I could in the swiftest manner – no more nice chatting. At this point I wasn't even aware that the oil had only been 'hot'.

I released my left arm to reach for the back door, which was off the kitchen. It was locked but I managed to undo it with one hand while holding her with the other: a skill I had originally mastered as a teenage boy with bra straps in the local cinema. I couldn't open it all the way as there was a waist-high unit by the wall, which I managed to knock out of place so that it was stopping the door from opening fully.

I was shuffling and slipping in the spilt oil towards the back door while keeping Nuts constrained with one arm; her voice had suddenly become very deep.

"Me no go now, me go later! YOU VERY BAD MAN!"

I was trying to pull her towards the door when, all of a sudden, we came to a halt. One minute we were moving along at a snail's pace in some kind of manic, slow motion waltz; next it was like I was Geoff Capes trying to pull a coach-load of elephants up a hill.

I tried again – nothing. We weren't going anywhere.

I finally noticed that Nuts' ultra-clean hand (obviously washed clean of any natural oils) was clamped in a vice-like grip on the corner of the wall that separated the kitchen from the rear lobby where the back door was.

I didn't want to let go of her in her current state, with all those implements of torture within reach and I didn't want to 'hurt' her to get her out of the house.

Another stalemate with me fresh out of ideas for a third time!

In all the commotion, we both failed to notice that someone else had come into the room.

Simon, who had heard the racket from upstairs, had wandered down to see Nuts and me in this very unlikely embrace.

Simon is about my height, but much wider and a keen gym rat. He's the sort of guy you would definitely want on your side if it all kicked off.

I quickly explained the situation and, like Robin to Batman, he took over holding Nuts while I called the police.

Nuts had let go of the wall and was now just outside the back door.

Both she and Simon were pushing against opposite sides of the door, but Simon, who has a very impressive bench press, couldn't quite close it. Nuts didn't have a foot in it or anything; she'd just summoned a huge amount of strength from her latent superpowers.

I tried to speak to the operator as calmly as possible whilst also keeping an eye on what was happening. It was difficult, but I managed to tell the operator where we were and what had just transpired.

I was told someone was on their way and looked round to see a bewildered Simon wondering how Nuts had got under *his* arm and back in the house.

She'd picked the frying pan up again and was waving it about at us.

I shouted at her to put it down. Forgetting I'd still got my phone to my ear, I jumped when the operator said in a calm voice,

"There is someone on their way, sir."

Nuts eventually put the frying pan down and ran back into the lounge. We both followed her in, puffing, fed-up, but with adrenalin pumping; both slightly embarrassed by our lack of success.

She was now waving a large phonebook at us, which although heavy looking, was probably the least harmful thing she could have picked up.

She then started wailing – I mean *really* wailing. A sound like which I have never heard in my life: relentless, loud and unstopping. She even had to sit down to give this hideous noise her full attention.

This went on for a full ten minutes without any let up. It was like fifteen car alarms all going off at once. She must have been taking oxygen in through her ears as she didn't seem to have taken a breath for ages.

A police car eventually pulled up outside. Nuts saw it and disappeared up the stairs.

Two police officers rushed in and we filled them in on what had happened.

By this time there was a pain growing in my stomach. I've got a hiatus hernia combined with an acid-producing machine of a stomach. These two 'tag team' during times of stress, after eating spicy food and too much physical exertion. I wondered what could have possibly triggered this bout; surely there are no spices in a caramel slice!

The police listened to what had happened but had already been filled in by the emergency operator. They asked me if I wanted her arrested but I told them I just wanted her out.

Nuts was locked in the bathroom and still screaming.

"Me no come out, no deposit!" to one of the officers who was telling her that he would break the door down if she didn't come out.

She finally opened the door and I told them exactly which pocket on her rucksack she had put the deposit in. The officer confirmed this.

Nuts was still refusing to leave, but both Simon and I had met our match so were happy to leave this to the professionals. Just as it looked like they might be reaching a stalemate, a call came through on the radio that an officer was down a couple of miles away.

The police, now eager to leave, physically removed Nuts from the house, told me to lock the door, which I double-locked, and wished me all the best.

I thanked them and Simon, waited five minutes and then headed down the road, dazed, confused and with no time for a change of clothes, to meet Jack. Man, want a morning!

...In the original version of *House Share Hero*, this is where this story ended.

It didn't really end here and actually got much more eventful, but due to some potential legal constraints, I couldn't really go on any more.

By the time you're reading this, the dust will have settled enough to really fill you in on how this panned out and it will be well worth a read.

As the days and weeks followed, the rest of these events involved more police intervention, the drug squad, a major car crash and an internal fraud investigation. To find out how this story really ended, visit **Housesharehero.co.uk** for the final piece of the jigsaw!

CHAPTER TWO

THE EVOLUTION OF THE HOUSE SHARE HERO

November 11th 1997: To my knowledge, not a monumental day in world history, but it was the day I stood in my 'slightly shabby' dining room, in my 'slightly shabby' house in a 'slightly shabby' street in a 'slightly shabby' part of town, opened a 'legal looking' letter and unwittingly launched my career as the 'House Share Hero'.

I didn't look much like a hero. I was twenty-three years old, 5ft 7 and didn't have wavy blond hair or a chiselled jaw. I was at least thirty pounds overweight, stuck in a dead end job earning less than £10k a year. It was a job I didn't really like and to which I had to travel forty-five minutes on some stinking bus to get to. To top it all off, I was broke beyond belief.

If someone had told me then that within about ten years I would be renting out seventy-four rooms, ten garages, three houses, two flats and have one of my properties featured on BBC news as the 'top end' of house shares in the area, I would have accused them of having a laugh!

If they'd also predicted that I would be living in a nice detached house with a lovely family, in a great area, with an ever changing choice of cars on the drive, start and finish work when I liked, have cash in the bank, and wouldn't need to do anything to achieve this for another six years, I would probably have punched them!

Anyway, back to 1997.

Although I didn't have much, two things I did have back then were:

HouseShareHero.co.uk

1. Absolute desperation
2. A house (I still have the house)

The letter I had opened confirmed to me that my ex girlfriend's name was now off the joint loan we had taken out exactly a year before to buy the house, and that I was left to pay the mortgage, endowment, a loan (which I'd got to pay her off), the ever-growing credit card my bank had given me for 'emergencies' and a whole host of other bills which my salary nowhere near covered.

My physical, mental and financial predicament could only be described in three words – on its arse!

Then, almost immediately, I had three amazing turns of fortune.

The first came from my best friend, Neil. He had just bought a house and decided that, rather than pay the mortgage himself, he would rent a couple of rooms out. Neil is a shrewd character, so much so that he would turn the heating off whenever he went out, to keep his bills down, even when his housemates were at home. I think he also banned any light bulbs over forty watts! I worked out that renting a room or two out myself, as Neil was doing, would considerably help my financial situation.

The second was meeting Julie; her misfortune became my lucky break. She had just split with someone too, got a job in the 'corporate Tenko' where I worked and needed a place to live.

She was bright, friendly, clean, and fitted neatly into my spare room. I worked out half the mortgage and added £50 and she agreed to pay it each month – result!

My dad, an old school West Indian who had come over to England in the sixties, got wind of this and called to give me a shrewd piece of advice. He had recently been through a divorce and seemed surprised to have come off worst in the case.

"Steevan (pause), even if she offer it to you, do not take it! You

26

will never get her out of the house if you do."

This troubled my naive young mind, so I decided to discuss it with Julie. She assured me that if I were the last man on earth, or she was desperate for some love, or the continuation of humanity depended on us getting it on – I would still be safe!

I was relieved, but must say very slightly insulted.

Incidentally, about a year or so later, my dad called to say that he had taken in a lodger and was having trouble getting rid of her.

I said, "Did you take it?"

There was a long pause, followed by a sigh before he said, "Yes Steevan."

Julie also turned out to be a potential lifesaver. She thought it was slightly odd that we both felt drowsy most evenings, especially when the 'antique' gas fire was in use. (Can you see where this is going?) I chose to ignore this observation and was livid when Julie got a gas engineer in to check things out. My anger soon turned to relief when he discovered that the fire was pumping out carbon monoxide, which at the time I thought only killed old ladies and kittens. There was also a serious gas leak. It transpired that boilers age like dogs and a twenty-year-old boiler should have been put down a long time ago!

My third piece of luck came from meeting Jez. He was bigger and older than Julie and me, a proper adult! Even if he did play with models ('cast iron' types not 'cast in films' types).

Jez slept a lot, could reach high things, was great to have around and we became the city's own mini version of 'friends'.

It was only a two-bed house, so Jez had the lounge as a bedroom. This was handy for him as he was quite lazy, and it limited the amount of times he had to use the stairs. We used the dining room as a lounge; I was lucky enough to have a breakfast room, which then became the dining room.

And that was that. I could still barely afford to feed myself (not sure where all the money went), didn't have a car and my debts were still growing, but I was a landlord with two great housemates who are still two of my best friends today.

By 2000, my girlfriend and later wife-to-be was now living with me, along with my current housemates, Ian and Robin. Ian was an up-and-coming stockbroker who had travelled down from Scotland to work locally, and Robin, who was much less dynamic and worked in an office where his desk faced a wall. Both were great guys. I still see Robin every now and again and, like Julie and Jez, Ian is one of my best mates.

Working in the head office of a travel agency meant that there were always people looking for places, so I had various lodgers from around the world living with me over the years: tall ones, short ones, fat ones, thin ones, pretty ones and pretty ugly ones. Some that liked to dress up as Vikings, some that were keen to watch late night telly and make the shower smell funny! There were those I fell out with; those who fell out with me. There was one who lived only on baked beans, jacket potatoes and Harry Potter books. There was even a girl who paid her rent like clockwork yet must not have stayed more than ten nights for the whole six months she was there.

On the one hand, I was stuck in the financial trap of having a house I couldn't quite afford, nor was clever enough to manage financially. On the other hand, and unbeknownst to me, for four years, I had not only been making great friends and meeting some terrific characters, but had been honing my skills as a landlord and gradually evolving as the House Share Hero.

My girlfriend and I moved into a house together in 2001. She bought it in her name, as my income was levied against my house. I was earning a heady £15k a year working as a 'Personal Account

Manager' in a high street bank. My old house was making a small amount of money with the three housemates I had in there. Life was easier, but I wasn't really getting anywhere. . .

It was time to use my superpowers!

CHAPTER THREE

STRIKING SUB PRIME GOLD

Suzie and I lived happily in her house for a couple of years, while Ian, Robin and Mike lived in my old house a few streets away. They all paid their rent like clockwork and it covered the mortgage and utility bills. I prayed that nothing would break down, or that I wouldn't be able to find good people to live there in the future.

By mid 2003, I had learned some very good sales skills at the bank. I would go on as many courses that I could as these kept me out of the branch, but this had the unexpected side effect that I was actually learning something. I had also reviewed enough people's bank accounts to realise that most of the 'high rollers' I would see out on a Friday night, and used to envy, were actually broke, and I was the one lending them the money for all the material glory with which they surrounded themselves. I had also worked out that, for most people, there were basically two types of consumer debt.

Revolving Debt: (credit cards, overdrafts, store cards, etc) which are extremely lucrative for financial institutions as the interest rates are generally quite high. In most cases, the rates were also 'variable' which meant the lender could change them at will. They would normally ask you to pay 'just a little' each month, meaning the debt 'revolved' for years and years if you weren't careful. This meant people were still paying for meals that had long since passed through them, clothes that were now well out of fashion, gifts for people they no longer liked and many other things they couldn't remember buying.

I'm embarrassed to say that on several occasions I exceeded 500% of my monthly credit card sales target, telling people to use them for emergencies only or, when they were in a place they didn't know, to protect against fraud. After all, if someone spent a £1000 on your credit card, it wouldn't be too bad while the bank sorted it, but if they spent a £1000 on your debit card and the money came out of your current account, think of the chaos that would cause! Also, what if your wallet got stolen on holiday? Just take this shiny, harmless piece of gold-coloured plastic and put it in the hotel safe – just in case.

I would then talk to them about the necessity of payment protection insurance and, before the ink was dry on the forms, I would make a note in my diary to call them in a year's time to pay it off with some:

Fixed Debt: usually in the form of a loan. For some reason money is a 'taboo' subject in our society. Schools and parents don't educate children about money and it's left to SALES advisors in financial institutions to do it. People like me who could be selling credit cards, loans, cars, houses, mobile phones, etc. And, like the guy on the high street who sold you your last phone or car, we all got a commission. Of course a bank couldn't be seen as paying its staff commission so they called it a 'bonus' instead. I would get great rewards for getting you into debt and in most cases nothing for opening you a savings account and encouraging you to put a 'bit by' each month in case the boiler packed up. So after Mr or Mrs Customer had got in trouble with his or her 'bucking bronco' of a credit card, I would invite him back in, rub my chin and tut like a mechanic looking under the bonnet of their broken car and then set them up with a 'retired pit pony' of a loan. A fixed rate, fixed term, fixed monthly payment solution to their problems. All very sedate and with no surprises. We'd throw in a bit on top of what they needed for the relaxing holiday they deserved after all of the stress that credit card had caused. Maybe something similar to the one, very poorly disguised as a 'team building' event, I'd just come back from, which the bank had sent me on as a thank you for all my 'Good Customer sales, I mean advice' I had given out for the last quarter.

With the card clear, I would lower the limit and tell him this time 'emergencies only!'

Now, where's my diary?

In time, I realised what the bigger picture was and what I and thousands of advisors were doing. I then dropped from the very top of the bank sales leagues to so far off the bottom that they didn't even bother spelling my name right half the time.

I was guiding people into the same situation I was once in. This wasn't just something that was affecting the poor and the stupid; I was meeting people with highflying careers and huge status within the community who had six-figure 'consumer debts' on credit cards, loans and car finance – not to mention the massive mortgages they were also trying to prop up. At least they spoke well, drove nice cars and had lovely houses.

Another holiday from the bank was now a distant pipe dream and my income was also starting to suffer. Although my old house was paying for itself, I was having trouble paying my half of the bills on the house I shared with Suzie. I needed some swift action.

The memories of being broke were still fresh in my mind – so fresh that they scared me witless, so I needed to do something quickly, very, very quickly.

For some reason this lead me to the 'self help' section of my local bookshop. I couldn't remember the last book I had read as an adult; I am not sure I ever did, but I left with two books: *The Seven Habits of Highly Effective People* by Dr Stephen Covey and *Rich Dad Poor Dad*, by Robert Kiyosaki. I picked the first book because it said 'Over 10 million copies sold' on the cover and the second because it was shiny and had fewer pages. I bought a bookmark so that I could keep them nice and either take them back to the shop, give them away as presents or sell them on Ebay.

Little did I know I was holding two great new 'Superhero'

powers in my hand and these two books would always remain as dog-eared trophies on my book shelf.

First came the realisation that my life was about choices and not 'needs', 'must do's and 'have to's. A simple way of explaining this is that you don't HAVE TO look both ways to cross a road; however, it's perhaps wise to 'CHOOSE TO' so you don't get hit by a bus or something similarly hard.

Knowing that life is about choices and not compulsive needs was essential for opening my mind to what I could achieve.

I also learned about the importance of inputs over outputs. The end result isn't where you should be putting your effort in; it's what gives you the end result that counts. For example: brushing and flossing your teeth (inputs) gives you a nice white shiny smile (output); if you had to cycle ten miles a day to work, it would take up a lot of your time; if you were lucky enough to be given a car (input) and drove, you would do it in a fraction of the time. More time and comfort are now your end result (output). But if you don't look after the car (input), it will break down and you will soon be back on your bike and lose your end result (output). If you don't look after your bike, then you'll be walking, sunshine, and in an even worse state!

It was clear that my customers were the 'input' and the bit of cash and growing asset I was getting in return were my 'end result' or 'output'.

I also learned that an 'asset' puts money in your pocket (however small or large an amount) and a liability takes money out of your pocket (however small or large). My rental property was an asset; the bills I was struggling with on the house I lived in with Suzie were a 'liability'.

I needed a big enough asset to cover this newly-realised liability!
I decided to buy another house!

The main problem with this brilliant idea was that I had no money. Although by now I had no consumer debts, my bank account was generally £50 either side of zero by the end of each month and savings were still a pipe dream.

I'd been to see a mortgage advisor who told me that not only would I need 15-25% deposit for a buy-to-let mortgage, I was probably breaking the terms of my current mortgage conditions by renting it out and not informing the lender. Oh crap!

With a heavy heart and light pocket, I left and phoned my mortgage company to see what their views were 'just in case' I ever wanted to rent my property out. To my surprise, they said it was no problem and if I gave them £100 they would even put it in writing for me!

With this crisp letter in my grubby hand, I practically ran back to the mortgage broker and asked him what he thought it meant.

Once again, he said I would need a large deposit for a buy-to-let, but my new shiny piece of paper meant I was free to get another residential mortgage on a house for me to live in, and there were even lenders who would lend me 100% or more of the value of a house to do so. The main downside would be that I would be exposing myself heavily to the risk of negative equity and also that it would be a 'residential' mortgage so I would have to live in any property I found.

I didn't really hear the last part as my mind had gone house hunting!

By chatting to agents, it became clear that the housing market, like most things in general, is split roughly into three: 'prime', 'average' and 'sub prime'

It also became clear that I could get up to 50% more house for my money in a 'sub prime' area than an 'average' one and nearly 100% more than in a 'prime' area of the city. I couldn't afford to buy in the prime areas anyway and the average areas wouldn't give me a good enough return.

From my own humble entry into the world and for the first few months of life, Mum and I lived in a small West London council bedsit nineteen floors up in a block of flats. When I was seven, we moved to a more rural part of the country with my step-dad into a new 'luxury' council estate.

As a kid growing up on council estates, you become acutely aware of how easily they are to get around on your BMX, where the cars can't go, the shortest way to your mate's house, the quickest way to the shop, where all the unsavoury characters were likely to be, so you didn't get your bike nicked or relieved of your A-team action figures.

Now that I was searching for a new rental property, I knew for a fact that there were prime, average, and sub prime council estates and that these areas remained relatively constant. For my search, I labelled these Gold, Silver and Bronze. One thing I didn't know, but learnt very quickly, was that a house on a 'bronze' council estate was about the same or only fractionally different in price to one on a 'silver' or 'gold' one.

I was also realising that my 16k Sinclair Spectrum brain would answer any question I put to it, so I asked it, "How can I find the silver and gold in all this bronze?"

It gave me four answers, along with my next Super-power:

Double-glazing, Ford Focuses, rat-runs and shoe leather.

Double Glazing:

The ex council properties I was looking at were originally built with wooden-framed windows. These houses were around twenty-five to thirty years old and in most cases the local council would paint or repair them in preference to replacing them with UPVC.

So double-glazing on a property generally meant that someone owned it. I also realised that where you had a lot of owned properties, then the areas were quite often looked after well, or very well, as those residents cared about the place where they lived and nearly always had a greater sense of community. There was also the 'keeping up with the Joneses' element, which meant 'if my neighbour has it then, I'd better get it!' It followed that people who owned these houses would nearly always have jobs so were both 'mortgageable' and 'employable'. From my experience of growing up on bronze, silver and gold estates, I felt I could almost read these areas like books and feel the residents' hopes, fears and aspirations as they were the same as my own and my family's had been.

There is a big word of caution here too! Sometimes I would see a couple of neighbours with the same double-glazing and it would be obvious that one had found a 'good guy' to install it, so the bloke next door and the girl across the road had used the same service.

More commonly these days, you will see rows or several houses with the same glazing. I found out, thankfully never to my peril, that this occurs when the council have realised that the windows need much more than a bit of paint and some filler and have done a 'job lot' of double-glazing – ahh, Kryptonite!

Ford Focuses:

I found Sunday evenings were best for this one as it's when most people are at home. Cars can also tell you a lot about an area. I'm not referring to whether or not they are on bricks (although this is a useful indicator), I'm talking about how old they are and what condition they're in. I found that the silver and gold areas generally had three to five-year-old, mid-size family cars parked on their streets (or slightly older people-carriers or family saloons, for instance) and they were, in most cases, kept clean. There was even the occasional zero to two-year-old 'sparkler', which I assumed (rightly or wrongly) to be financed, or belonging to a company giving more credence to these people's credit worthiness and employment status.

My theories here were also substantiated by my double-glazing finds.

Rat Runs:

During the day, these are great to get places on your bike, to play hide and seek, or take a shortcut to your mate's house. But at night, more ideal for legging it with stolen laptops, DVD players, dodging the old bill and generally using them as 'mini crime highways' with no speed limits.

With this in mind, I concentrated on properties that had either none or very few of these alleyways nearby, and were on the edges of areas where there was no real reason to come to that part of the estate unless you lived there. These houses had to also have wide, well-lit pathways running by them.

Strangely enough, these places were also higher in Ford Focuses and double-glazing!

Shoe leather:

This is probably the most important Superpower of them all. I found I could cover ground more thoroughly and investigate the above best, by walking round the areas and chatting to a few locals.

In general, most places are safe, most of the time and, if an area isn't right, it should be quite obvious.

I normally start by going round during the daytime and in the car. If I like the area I'll go back again and have a walk around, checking out exactly where gold or silver becomes bronze and looking for reasons why.

I'll then go round three or four times more, during the purchase process, at different times of the day and evening to make sure my initial thoughts were correct.

I was once in an area that I had already discounted for investment but, for some reason, was still walking around, smugly reinforcing my theories to myself, when I came across a teenage girl and four or five young lads. She was singing what I thought seemed like a childish rhyme. It wasn't until I got near them that I realised she was singing, "Rah, Rah, Rah, Rah, Rah, we're gonna F—king do Yah!"

I decided that if things did kick off I would start with the biggest one to try and make a stand. I quickly identified the lad, at least six inches taller than me but quite lanky. Neither a great lover nor a fighter, I decided I'd go for his middle and try to double him up if things got messy.

As I walked casually past them, this lovely lass shouted out, "MUG 'im!"

I spun round, ready to execute my plan of attack. I looked the lad straight in the eye (immediately thinking I should have picked the second biggest). He looked back at me and then to my ultimate surprise, looked down at his feet.

I looked at two of the others and they were doing the same. The remaining one then picked up his bike and just rode off.

The girl was still frantically screaming, "MUG 'im, MUG 'im!" But they just weren't having it.

I walked casually and cautiously back past the group, dark alleyways, rusty Ford Escorts and broken wooden-framed windows, without a trace of smugness, and fumbled my keys in the lock of the car. I started the car after locking the doors and drove home with the sound of my heart beating in my ears drowning out the radio.

I own an ex council house less than 150 yards from that area, which could not be more different. All that separates them is a single carriageway road that, from a psychological point of view, might as well be a 100 foot wall.

The only other time I got really scared was when I came across a group of people dressed in long black trench coats and one was holding a handgun.

Once again I had been smugly proving my theory right, had stayed too long and ventured too far into the wrong place.

The lads looked relatively harmless and I'm sure the gun was a toy or fake rather than real; after all, it was 1.pm on a Sunday for goodness sake!

I still made a calm but hasty retreat.

CHAPTER FOUR

THE HOUSE

With my first house-share still ticking along nicely, but my pockets feeling bottomless when it came to finding any cash in them, I finally found my house.

Four-bedroom, ex-council houses seemed to be my best choice and I realised that, in my city, there were about six different designs for these, in a variety of two and three storeys.

I decided not to go for a traditional two storey house as I wanted double bedrooms and could only find these types of houses with two, maybe three doubles at best. They also had large gardens and I couldn't envisage the sharers cutting the grass!

Of the several types of three storey places I came across, one sort was perfect!

The ground floor comprised a large kitchen-diner of 20'x12', a cloakroom and bedroom approximately 12'x10'. In the middle and directly above the kitchen-diner was a very large living room, again 20'x12' along with another 12'x10' bedroom. There were two even bigger bedrooms on the top floor along with a bathroom – all in all a large solid unit!

After looking at a few of these, I managed to find one that the owner wanted to sell quickly and got a good price. It was also within ten minutes of my own house, which I had decided was crucial, giving the amount of time I would be going backwards and forwards to it.

To this day, I have always stuck to the same technique and all of my rental units are within a song or two on the radio from where I live.

I went to see my mortgage advisor and found a loan company who agreed to lend with 105% of the purchase price. I didn't have any money for legal fees, or stamp duty and I wanted to do a bit of work on the place so I practically bit his hand off.

The purchase went along smoothly; on the day of completion I not only got the keys to my new asset but also a few thousand pounds in the bank.

I didn't need to question my desire to own this property, as my banking background told me that mortgage debts work well in most cases because the buyer generally has to put in a deposit. Although small compared to the value of the property – say 5, 10, or 15% – it was a large enough sum to ensure the buyer had thought things through properly, and would also be very motivated to hang onto the place if things got difficult.

Generally, raising money to pay solicitors, stamp duty, and let alone raising a deposit requires going through some pain. It might be a small twinge like using an inheritance or trust fund, or a large one, such as having to sell an asset or get a second job to save up the money, while having to live on baked beans on toast for a year. Nevertheless, in most cases you fully appreciate the money that has left your pocket to acquire your new 'bricks and sticks'. Just being able to sign next to the 'X's then getting the keys plus cash does not do most people any favours.

But hey – what did I know about those sorts of things compared to clever fellows in their suits and corner offices?

A week after completion, I phoned my new mortgage lender and asked if I could let out the property. I thanked them for their help in buying the place and said I now didn't want to live there, but neither did I want to sell it and could not afford to keep it empty.

At the time, the best 'buy to let' mortgage available from this lender (and any other for that matter) would require me to put at least 15% down. I had put -5% down: a massive 20% less than their minimum 15%!

I was sure they would say, "On yer bike son". I know I would have done. But instead, they agreed! Their only conditions were that I must always use an assured short hold tenancy and I could not put any people in who were on housing benefit. They were even very apologetic for the £100 I had to send them to cover the administration charges for putting this in writing to me!

RESULT!!

They had made no stipulation in the letter as to whether or not I could rent it out as a house-share and I chose not to bring it up. Why rock the boat? All they insisted was that I always used a tenancy agreement and that my minimum lease would be for six months and no more than twenty-four.

Every night I would be out of the bank at 4:57.pm and across town in my polyester suit, straight to the house, to do some painting or odd jobs and get the place shipshape for letting. My bank suit was ideal; not only did it mean I didn't have to buy one, it was also extremely stain resistant. You could cover it in paint, sawdust, or wood glue and nothing would stick to it or damage it. It was like the black box on a plane: indestructible!

I also had a builder in to put a wall up in the middle of the living room on the middle floor, making it into two medium sized doubles. Conveniently, the room ran from the front to back of the house and already had a window at each end, as well as lights, so that the conversion was very easy and not too expensive.

The ground floor bedroom now had a couple of sofas in and made a good sized living room. Along with the large kitchen diner, the downstairs now looked like a very traditional house. There were three double bedrooms on the middle floor and two on the top, giving me a large five-bed house. This added value to the place and within a few months I was able to transfer it into a traditional 'buy to let' using the equity as a deposit.

As it was a house-share, not only did I pay the mortgage but all the utility bills as well. It worked out nicely that three of the sharers would cover these costs and the other two would be profit. I was satisfied that I could keep the place at least 60% occupied but was over the moon when, in the first year, and most years after that I maintained over 90-95%. These days it operates somewhere between 97-100%

There were, however, four major mistakes that I made in my exuberant inexperience.

The first one was failing to check the boiler. It was old and about as reliable as a high five from a blind guy on a trampoline. A costly item to replace but, luckily, I had got a good deal on the house to start with. The next was installing an extra shower in an upstairs airing cupboard: a nice touch but not essential as a large percentage of my sharers in those areas worked shifts, so that getting into the bathroom was not really a huge problem, plus there was a cloakroom downstairs.

The third, most costly, and biggest mistake was in massively underestimating the quality of person I could get to live in the house. I initially found three great guys, who I really liked, to move in almost immediately and, somewhat unprofessionally, made the mistake of being slightly too friendly with – an old habit from my own sharing days, but then the last two rooms didn't let straight away.

I now have the maturity as a landlord to know that an empty unit will only cost me money, whereas letting the wrong person move in will, in most cases, not only cost me money in the form of rent arrears, damage, and excess wear and tear, but also loss of sleep, time, reputation and massively increased anxiety!

The house was paying for itself and the rooms had only been empty a couple of weeks but, with a mixture of inexperience, greed, and arrogance, I let one of the rooms to Tina and the other to Wayne. With the house full I was ready to put my feet up.

How naive could I be?

Tina was 19, scrawny-looking, with teeth so yellow that I couldn't believe they weren't butter. She was barely working and immediately lost her mysterious job as soon as she moved in. She had a male friend in his mid forties helping her financially. In fact she seemed to have several, slightly sheepish, middle-aged male friends, dropping by regularly, who seemed to be giving her a few quid.

People's kindness never ceases to amaze me.

Her attitude was generally stroppy and I normally avoided being alone with her as she made me itch. She was a heavy smoker and, although not in the house, had that horrible 'old smoke' smell about her. On one occasion, I was visiting one of her housemates and we were chatting in the kitchen, when Tina came in, bent over to get a bin bag from under the sink and we were both witness to her stringy, incredibly dirty, disgusting thong! I had trouble sleeping that night.

Over a very short period, her already 'wrong side of average' appearance worsened considerably and most of her 'special friends' stopped visiting. The ones that were left looked worse than she did.

In those days, I naively collected the rent each Friday from a 'rent box' with a slot in it that I had screwed to the wall. Tina and Wayne were the only ones in the house when everyone's rent was mysteriously fished out of it. They each blamed the other and, as I trusted neither of them, it was hard to pinpoint which one it was. The fourth lesson I learned about making people pay by standing order or rent book now saves me much more time and effort, so it was a good, but rather expensive one.

Just as I was about to evict her, Tina suddenly announced that she was pregnant and somehow managed to find herself a hostel which was a relief all round. She went without saying goodbye to anyone or taking anything with her.

Her stuff was essentially worthless, but a lot of it would have had great sentimental value. I bagged it up carefully and put it in the shed, where it stayed for over a year, but she never came back for any of it. Her phone had been cut off but I tried to get word to her that, although she owed me a few hundred quid, I wanted her to have her personal items back, such as, family photo's, cards and gifts, etc. The messages either didn't get to her or she didn't want the items. I eventually heard that she had left town, so got rid of it all.

About two years after she had moved out, I saw her picture on the front of the local paper. She had somehow got off a bus forgetting her kid and was trying to blame the bus company for it!

Wayne, believe it or not, was an even bigger problem than Tina. He was either running at 100mph or barely conscious. This turned out to be from a cocktail of prescribed, over the counter, and 'from a bloke down an alley' drugs he was taking.

From the work I had done on the house, there was about a tonne of rubble and other items to get rid of. As the house was in a pedestrianised area, with the nearest place to put a skip 100 metres away, getting rid of it was going to be inconvenient and not very cheap.

Wayne, who had only been there a couple of days, and hadn't yet raised any alarm bells, offered to get rid of it all for £20. Result! That afternoon I got a call from the neighbour to say that she couldn't get out of her front door. My house was an end terrace with a neighbour one side; her house was next to mine but set back, with her front door adjacent to my side gate.

It transpired that Wayne had driven his car along the pedestrianised pathway and reversed over her immaculate front garden, stopping with the passenger side about an inch from her front door. He had then loaded his car up, which had a 750cc engine, with over a tonne of rubble and had been surprised when it had sunk into her rose garden. Tired and slightly distressed from all this effort, he had then decided to go the pub for the rest of the day.

I managed to get hold of him and, in his now half-cut state, he promised he would rectify this immediately.

To his credit, an hour later, the only evidence of his car, the rubble and all the commotion was next door's front carnage – I mean garden – and two muddy tyre tracks leading off into the distance.

I went round the next day to tell him off, pay him his twenty quid and apologise to next door.

He seemed genuinely sorry and the back garden now looked spotless, so I decided it must have been a 'one off'. Yeah, right!

While all the rubble had gone, there was still a large pile of wood I had inherited from the previous owner that Wayne said he would shift for £10. He seemed keen to have another chance and almost drooled when I gave him the tenner in advance.

I left, nervous but happy.

That afternoon, my builder, who had just started tiling the new shower room, called to say that there was a large fire going on in the back garden with some bloke running around trying to put it out with pint glasses full of water – WAYNE!

He had switched his phone off, so I told the other housemates to let him know that I would be coming over in the morning to have a long talk with him and discuss our options. Stupidly, when Wayne had moved in, I'd forgotten to bring a tenancy agreement with me, so he didn't have one. I would just have to bluff this one.

By now, Wayne had got the impression that I wanted him out, and had gone down the chemist, back alley, then pub to drown his sorrows and help give him inspiration as to how he was going to make things up to me.

When I arrived the next morning, I was greeted by seven people.

ONE Wayne, bursting with excitement at the 'great deeds' he had accomplished overnight.

FOUR housemates who hadn't slept a wink all night due to the commotion.

ONE builder demanding to know where all his tools and tiles had gone.

ONE irate neighbour, acting as spokesperson for several other irate neighbours, who felt they could not be held accountable for their actions if they came face to face with me. Yes, the first neighbour was the lady with the wrecked garden from next door.

I also had a letter from the council asking me if I was running a HMO (House in Multiple Occupancy) and, if so, why didn't I have a licence for it.

To top it off, the new(ish) lounge carpet was missing and it looked as if Ray Charles and Stevie Wonder had been in to tile the kitchen.

Since I had last spoken to Wayne the night before and, after returning from the pub via several other places, he had spent the night 'red-lining'. Not only had he thrown the lounge carpet away because it was 'mouldy', (It wasn't mouldy; it turned out that, like a puppy, he had somehow got over-excited and soiled himself on it.) he had also taken it upon himself to re-tile the kitchen which, incidentally, happened to be already tiled.

Due to the fact that he was using the tiles meant for the shower room, he had run out about halfway round. Determined that this minor setback wouldn't stop him, he had then scoured the house, garden and street for bits of plastic, old scraps of wood, plasterboard, etc. so that he could continue with his masterpiece: basically anything he could find, that he could move and that was reasonably flat (It didn't matter how thick it was.) was now attached to my kitchen wall. Even a wooden chopping board!

Shortly after this and with daylight approaching, his speed had dropped to about 90 mph. He had no money and the people he had been dealing with didn't take IOU's. He had somehow managed to find someone at 5.am interested in buying a few 'used tools' so was now feeling fine again. And, it would also seem generous, as he winked at me and told me I didn't owe him any money for his night's work.

I must have had the same look on my face as the people on *Changing Rooms* used to have after a 'bad reveal' when their once slightly dull living room now resembled an Amsterdam brothel. I was opened-mouthed yet completely speechless.

I turned to the neighbour, who genuinely looked sorry for me, and she said, "Do you know where the wheelie bins have gone for the three houses alongside this one?"

I sighed and said no. Wayne had also stopped smiling.

It transpired that they were now in the local pond full of rubble!

Wayne had been correct in his thinking that the rubble meant the bins would sink to the bottom of the pond, but hadn't taken into account that it was only two feet deep.

Just at that moment there was a gust of wind and a puff of cartoon smoke where Wayne had just been standing and he was gone.

I managed to catch up with him a few days later; he had moved his girlfriend in by this time and was surprisingly behind with his rent. A few mysterious fist-sized holes had also begun to appear in the walls.

They were skint, restless and, at the same time, lethargic. I offered them £100 to go that day, along with writing off their arrears and, as if by magic, they were gone forever.

The next door neighbour saw them leave and came round to thank me.

I apologised again and she gave me a doggy bag with some of the used condoms and 'sex stained' tissues they had been throwing out of their bedroom window and into her front garden.

I noticed there were still a couple of such items in her tree, but didn't think it was probably the best time to mention it.

I still see Wayne every now and again and he sometimes asks me if I have any places to rent.

Unfortunately, I'm always full.

Touch wood, the house has run very smoothly since.

CHAPTER FIVE

EYES OPEN

As soon as the dust had settled on my second house, I ran into my third.

It was exactly the same as my first one, but on the other side of town and timber clad. I later found out that it was also timber-framed, meaning it was essentially a three storey shed! Luckily, the roof was tiled and not felt.

By stroke of good fortune it was another end terrace so had at least one brick wall, which turned out to be a real bonus when changing lenders on it. For some strange reason, lenders didn't like houses without bricks in them but were generally happy so long as they had a few.

The location of this one was 'silver' within my 'sub prime' budget. It backed onto a church and some council bungalows for the over 50s. I took a gamble that neither group would be especially rowdy and bought the place. It was also on the edge of the estate with no through traffic, and beyond the church was a main road with a dual carriageway after that, so there was no reason to pass the house unless you lived nearby or were going to church.

I decided that this area didn't fit my 'gold' criteria as my investigations found that a year or so before, in the middle of this estate, someone had been murdered and his body left in the boot of a car. More recently, someone's arm had been chopped off with a machete. These incidents were sufficiently remote not to affect my house, but still close enough.

The local shopping centre hadn't been updated for about twenty-five years or so and, from my experiences growing up not too far away, along with Fridays and Saturday nights working as a

Special Constable a few years previously, I knew it wasn't a place to be after dark.

Again, the house was too far away from this to be a major concern, but it was still a considerable factor.

Before joining the Specials I had been quite shy and would often just blend into the background in whatever I did. Three years of seeing what the worst of the city had to offer – after all, no one calls the police when things are going well – was now really paying off with my property investment choices.

I knew what to look for in people and places; I knew where people had given me the slip or had a go at me, and I knew where the good working class areas were that had very little or no trouble, a neighbourhood watch committee and a strong sense of pride. When looking at the kids in the area, my powers could tell me whether their parents should be saving money for university or bail. My time on the beat had given me increased confidence and more of a willingness to explore the unknown.

It also meant that whatever I came across in my day-to-day life was generally not a patch on what I'd seen at 'chucking out time' over the weekend.

Depending on your point of view, it also had the benefit/hindrance that I was becoming more and more unemployable. How could my boss at the bank get me to wear some stupid badge with my name on it when I didn't want to? After all, I'd been abused, punched, kicked, chased and, on one occasion, knocked out. Some middle-aged, balding, polyester suit-wearing, corporate monkey wasn't going to get me to wear a cheap plastic badge saying 'I'm here to help'!

I was never rude, generally well-liked, and top or near the top of the sales leagues most of the time, so it was hard for them to discipline me. I stayed within the company rules, but it was on my terms.

However, I did cross the line when the local council started road works on a bridge between my house and the branch where I worked. Because they had reduced the number of lanes in use, it meant that I was now ten minutes late for work each day.

When my boss sighed at my monthly appraisal and said: "What am I going to do about this constant lateness?" I told him to take it up with the council.

I kind of knew then I was on borrowed time.

Incidentally, when the bridge did re-open, they made the lanes that were closed only accessible to buses and black cabs, so I was still late every day!

After I'd left the bank and was working for myself, all this sitting in traffic on 'my time' became irritating. I remedied this by buying a retired London Black Cab on eBay; not only was it a fine piece of British history, I was now flying round the city in the bus lanes!

Thorough investigations into the area where I was buying my third property, awarded me two important pieces of information.

One was that the local shopping centre had just been sold and would be undergoing a several million pound makeover within the next five years. Coincidentally, a similar development had just happened near my last house and had improved the area no end. The second was that almost all of the trouble in the area was being caused by two large feuding families. The council had finally had enough of them and rehoused them all a month or so earlier.

I also noticed that quite a few of the houses nearby either had ramps up to the front doors, or an extra step, along with hand rails either side of the door. My asthma had stopped me from joining the force full time and I doubt I would ever have made detective, but this feature, along with rows of net curtains, suggested that there was a thriving older population here.

I knocked on a few doors, spoke to a few people and confirmed that, since the troublesome families had been moved on, the area was now like 'the good old days' again and generally a good place to live.

But the reputation persisted, so I was able to get the house at a good price as the owner couldn't believe anyone would pay 'that much' for an ex council house. When the estate agent came round, she, along with most investors, didn't know that the problems locally had either been dealt with or were in hand; finally the seller looked desperate by listing it with too many agents.

Not only did it look like something was wrong with the place, it also meant that the estate agent would take a smaller bite of the commission cherry rather than risk losing it all. The agent told me the exact amount of money the seller required for the 'dream bungalow' which was to be her next home and that the vendor of this bungalow was getting twitchy and wanted things hurried up.

Coincidentally, the lowest price she could have taken was the price I ended up paying for it.

I was only able to get a 100% mortgage this time round; I did the same conversion as before, using the new increased value as a deposit, stuck it on a buy-to-let mortgage and moved some good people in.

Once again, the last couple of rooms stuck, but this time I was much more patient in filling them!

The only real problem I encountered with this house was that it was the lowest on the 'drainage' run and the lady six doors up had planted a lovely decorative bush in her front garden. Neither of these things would normally be a problem, but the roots of the bush had penetrated the waste pipe and it periodically blocked up. As my drain was the lowest on the run, the only symptom of the blockage would quite often be raw untreated sewage all over the front garden as the manhole cover was in the middle of the lawn!

The council and neighbours understandably thought it was my guys who were causing the problem and I was becoming unpopular. After visiting the place mid-blockage to find a group of kids dipping sticks in it, writing on walls and cars and flicking sweetcorn at each other, I paid to have a camera put down there and the problem was thus identified.

I never did get any money back for all the 'unblocking' that went on, but did learn about all the jabs you need to clear drains on a daily basis, how you can 'age' a blockage by the colour of what's down there (brown = new/ grey = old) and also that the human body has trouble digesting sweetcorn husks.

I was also learning that because of the many variables with property and people, along with the fact I'd never met anyone who could see into the future, there are only two types of so-called and often self-appointed 'Property Experts'. These are:

1. Those who don't know.
2. Those who don't know they don't know.

I decided that I was very comfortable with being in the first category and found myself listening to and learning more from people who would use words like, 'could', 'may' and 'should' and became less interested in those who were using words such as, 'will', 'always', 'definitely'.

I was slowly noticing that whenever the crap hit the fan, the people in the second category would often just disappear, blame everyone apart from themselves, or just say things like:

"I didn't think that would happen!"

"I'm as surprised as you are," or "Bye!"

When your train leaves for 'Crapville', other people can only go so far with you. When you take a trip – and all House Share Heroes do at some point – Crapville's population is one. And if you haven't guessed, that's you! When your train leaves town, all of your supporters will be there with you smiling.

Firstly, your advisors will get off but you've still got your friends and family. Then your friends will get off; they will smile, wave and genuinely wish you luck, but they've got their own problems.

Your close family will come right to the city limits; they will cry, worry, lose sleep, think about you twenty hours a day, but if you check your ticket, it will say, "Admit one".

You may think this is a sad view; you may completely relate to it. You may vehemently disagree, but you must try to understand it.

A couple of months after buying this house, with it ticking along nicely, I got a call from a guy called Malcolm.

Malcolm seemed like a nice chap and had got my number from a friend of a friend of a friend, who had told him what I was getting into. He was likeable but had been told by certain investors and estate agents that property value WOULD double every seven years, ALWAYS made people money and that good old-fashioned bricks and mortar was DEFINITELY the best and safest form of investment.

We met for a pint. I told him my story so far, put him right on a few points and he asked me if I would help him. In return, he would pay me to manage his houses so we would both make a few quid out of it.

I wasn't sure that Malcolm had 'the skills to pay the bills' but he did seem to have 'the heart to play the part' so I agreed. I gave him several books to read and told him to make sure he knew what he was getting himself into. I also gave him as much factual information as I could and made it clear that this way of investing wasn't easy unless you were very good at it. I gave him a whistle-stop tour of my places and told him that if I had known about the obstacles I would come up against beforehand I probably wouldn't have done it.

Malcolm seemed to be seeing pound signs at every conversational corner and noticeably 'glazed over' when anything negative was discussed.

Like me, Malcolm didn't have a deposit for a house but, unlike me, he did have a loan, for which he had to find several hundred pounds a month for the repayment. He told me that he could easily afford this loan and had never missed a payment. I gave him the numbers of some good Estate Agents and Mortgage Advisors, told him all I knew and wished him luck.

What Malcolm ended up with wasn't quite right, but workable. He had found a lender who would not only give him enough money to buy the house but also enough to clear his mammoth loan. This meant that even with no income from the house, he was still no financially worse off each month than he'd been before, but now owned a property.

Well I think he owned a property. He had borrowed 125% of its value so did he technically own -25% of it? Did this mean that a complete stranger who owned 0% of the place owned more than he did? The question seemed unanswerable and we both marvelled about how clever the people at Southern Stone bank were!

The only problem lay with the property he had bought. It was a two storey, four-bed with two doubles and two tiny singles. The price was OK but there was no way of adding any value to it, by fitting another bedroom in, without seriously reducing the size of the communal spaces. It was also clear that he hadn't read the books I had given him, and didn't have a clue what to do next.

Luckily for him, the lender granted permission for him to rent the place out and I tried to fill it for him. Due to the house having two very hard to let tiny single rooms and that there were only four rentable rooms instead of five, the next year Malcolm's cash flow from the property (income after all expenses) was anywhere between £100 - £300 per month. This was a healthy figure but could have easily been double with the right property.

I told him to pretend he still had the large loan so that he could save the cash flow along with an extra £500 per month to cover the deposit on the next place he was itching to buy.

What I didn't know at this point was that Malcolm was spending all of the income from his investment to the detriment of the utility bills and, some months, even the mortgage payments! He was now even talking about taking out a loan for a deposit on another place. I told him that this was an extremely risky strategy and something that most investors, especially a novice shouldn't even consider.

He seemed to have taken my comments on board, but within a week he called to say that he had borrowed enough for a deposit on another place. I told him to go straight back to the bank and cancel the loan as it had been arranged over the phone so, under the distance selling rules, had a cooling off period. Even if, in the unlikely event there were some fees to pay it would still be the best thing to do.

The next day he called back to say that he owed at least £5,000 more than the amount he had in his bank account, as the bank had also consolidated some other debts he didn't know he had. He was furious with his bank for taking advantage of him like that and was prepared to take the matter to the top.

"Even the omnuds... imsbudma... Homnutsma... bank Police!"

He had £15,000 in his bank account and was convinced that another property would solve all of his problems.

We reduced the size of the living room in his current house to incorporate another small single room to increase his income and I agreed to look for another house for him. I found one quickly but due to his now reduced credit rating, he would have to use the full £15,000 as a deposit. He was excited by this prospect, but called back an hour later to say there was only £13,000 in his account. I asked him where the other £2,000 had gone and he told me he had never had that amount and that I'd made a mistake. Maybe I had, who knew?

A week or so later I found a place that only needed £13, 000 to invest but he was now down to £11,000; this reduced to£9,000 then £7,000 over the next few months.

He had no real answers as to where this money was going, but was always tanned and never seemed short of a few quid. He was going abroad four or five times a year, had bought a Mercedes and I never saw him in the same clothes twice.

Bailiffs were now starting to turn up at his rental property even though the cash flow on it was positive. The people living there were getting understandably nervous.

After a disagreement, we parted ways and he decided to manage his place himself and, at the same, time put it up for sale.

We didn't stay in contact after that but I heard that Malcolm managed to find a buyer for his house before the bank repossessed it. I did hear that he bought a house like one of mine a couple of years later for about double what he had paid for the first one in a very 'bronze' area.

I've heard he still blames everyone else for what's happening to him, which is sad. Fingers crossed it goes well for him this time!

CHAPTER SIX

ASSETS AND LIABILITIES

By this time, I had exhausted my current *modus operandi* and my mortgage advisor didn't have any new ideas about buying houses without deposits. But, at about the same time, great deals were being offered to me left, right and centre. These were no more frequent than before, but my developing powers were making me more attuned to them.

For a few years now, the bank had been working hard to move more women into managerial roles within the organisation.

Banking had been historically male-dominated for centuries and the corporate structure had looked like a tree full of monkeys. The monkeys at the top looked down and all they could see were smiling faces looking up at them, whereas all the monkeys at the bottom could see when they looked up were arses. The bank had commendably decided that it was time to address this massive imbalance. A women's network had been set up a few years earlier, which had been hugely successful and the gaps between jobs, income and attitudes were rapidly being re-addressed.

To give the bank full credit, it also realised that there was the same imbalance when it came to ethnic minorities and senior positions. The tree was a lot browner at the bottom than it was at the top! They set up a network for all ethnic minorities who worked in the bank to try and deal with this. This theme became very close to my heart and even if I didn't like what I was doing very much on a day-to-day basis, I will always have the utmost respect for the bank and am even a shareholder!

It was also a day out of the office and a chance to meet like-minded people.

My boss scoffed at my invitation saying, "The bank doesn't need this sort of thing!"

He laughed when it said I could wear my national dress and wondered out loud if I should wear 'cricket whites' or a 'basketball' outfit.

Oh, the irony!

At one of these conferences, one of the United Kingdom's most famous Olympians was the final speaker. Not only was he full of energy and compelling to listen to, he was now also a successful businessman. However, at the end of his talk he stunned the audience into silence by flashing this on a twelve foot screen and declaring that for us:

'OPPORTUNITYISNOWHERE'

There were gasps, tuts and an overwhelming feeling of deflation from the thousand or so people in attendance. I could even hear anger in some of their mutterings.

After a few seconds of stunned silence, he pressed his clicker and the words separated to read:

'OPPORTUNITY IS NOW HERE'

Like an alcoholic hitting rock bottom, I suddenly had a moment of complete clarity.

Not only to what I had so far been doing by haphazard chance, but also as to how I would carry my business into the future and give me financial independence.

My hands were sore after clapping; I was the first to start and last to finish. I'm not religious in any way, shape or form but I felt like I had witnessed an epiphany!

I had suddenly gained three more powers:

1. The difference between first and last in a race can be less than half a second and the difference between first and second place can be so minute that you need to study a photograph in intricate detail to see who the winner really is. However, the difference in result is massive, whether it's money, status, recognition or fame. The person who is only fractionally better than the people around them will receive much more of what he or she wants than the person who is a millimetre behind them. It's true that people rarely remember who came second and that this can also be applied to any part of your work, financial or personal life.

2. Most people look at most things in the same light and, apart from a few small to medium hiccups along the way, I could now quantify the fact that what I was doing was looking at property investments slightly differently to most other investors. While novice and experienced landlords would categorise areas as 'good, average and bad' I was breaking my chosen investment area down even further and was seeing and understanding these areas in finite detail and with clarity. It was important to me that my houses and customers added value to an area, whether it was to the local economy or diversity of culture. My guys would be giving something back to these communities, not just adding density to the population and stripping it of resources. I'm now proud to say that, apart from very few exceptions, they actually do this.

3. I now had a precise vision of my goal. I didn't want a boss; I wanted to make all of the decisions. I also wanted my own wealth – not a fraction of the wealth that I was making for someone else. I wanted to live my life on *my* terms and no one else's. I now needed to get rid of the forty hours of the week I was selling to the 'the man' as soon as I possibly

could. Once I had this time back, I could use it to build my quality of life. By now, my net monthly income from the bank was about £1,500 per month: about a third higher than the average for my city but not enough to change my life. All I had to do was replace this 'forty hours a week' of earned income with three to six hours per week of 'rental income'.

When I'm not buying houses, my average monthly time spent per rental unit is about forty five minutes to an hour. Although I might spend a couple of hours a week on viewings on a few properties, most of my houses may not take any of my time at all. I will go into time management later on.

After hearing this talk from the great champion, I was truly inspired. On the train journey home, I made a promise to myself that I wouldn't be at the next annual conference. Not because I didn't enjoy them (they were the highlight of my year) but because, by hook or by crook, I would have left the rat race by then.

I was extremely sad that I missed the next conference, but felt slightly better when I found out that 90's three-hit wonder 'Apache Indian' was that year's guest speaker!

My eyes were now wide open and, with no real knowledge about how I was going to achieve this, nor with any major cash in the bank, I called every estate agent I knew in the city and told them I was ready to buy!

I charmed, flirted and schmoozed and the next day got a phone call to say that a chain involving nine houses was just about to collapse, as the person at the bottom had pulled out.

No one had bothered to check until the last minute whether he actually owned the property he was selling and, understandably, when his landlord found out, he had raised an objection.

The chain had already been plodding along for nearly a year and was now looking taught, tired and tenuous. The couple now at the bottom of the chain were expecting a baby in six weeks and their dream house, which happened to be in a stinker of an area, was slipping away fast.

House prices were also rising at a rate of knots and several of the people in the chain would now be unable to afford to buy the same or similar houses if it all fell through.

I had seen all the ex council four-bed footprints the city had to offer, along with all the three-beds, or so I thought. This one was a three storey three-bed.

On the ground floor was a large kitchen diner; there was a large lounge with conservatory off it and a cloakroom. The middle floor had two large doubles and a bathroom and, in what appeared to be a loft conversion, there was a very large bedroom. It was obvious that it wasn't an actual conversion but purpose-built. I had never seen this design before. It was in a row of six identical houses, on the edge of an estate, backing onto a large field with a busy road behind that. Once again there was no real reason to come near the area unless you were local to it and it was comparable to the other areas I had bought. There were more kids knocking about than I would have ideally liked, but they seemed well-behaved and I quickly built up a good rapport with them.

It was also obvious that I couldn't really change this house about too much. It just needed a lick of paint and a couple of carpets which wasn't going to increase its value much, meaning that any money I put into it would be stuck there, for at least the medium term.

It was about 10% below market value, which meant even if I could get 15% together and remortgage straight away, I would still have 5% stuck in it. Not a lot, I know, but it might have been 50% of the value, as I didn't have it. I asked myself if I could afford to buy this house and my 16k spectrum brain eventually gave me this answer.

"No, you idiot; this one will never work! You've got three houses so why don't you quit while you're ahead? You're not bright enough to make this work so why don't you leave it to the experts? Do better at your job and you might get a promotion in three years."

Thanks, Brain! Where was my great Olympic champion when I needed him? I went to bed sulking.

I woke up in the middle of the night for a pee. I knew drinking past 10.pm meant this was going to happen, but I did it anyway. Rather pointlessly, I was rebelling against myself, while lying there thinking, "Its cold outside of my duvet, can I hold this until the morning?" My ever-helpful brain booted up.

'Nope, I told you this would happen and now you must be punished; I'm not going to tell you where your dressing gown is and won't be reminding you that you left your gym bag in the middle of the hallway either.'

My brain and I have since been to counselling and I'm pleased to say have patched up our differences. We now work and play together very well and have even been on a few holidays.

While standing there, in the loo, marvelling at my semi-conscious aim with one arm against the wall, propping myself up, my brain said to me:

'Look, I know I've been hard on you. I will always answer any question you give me, so just ask me better questions. Tell me what you want and I'll tell you how to get there. Ask me rubbish questions and I'll give you rubbish answers'.

I said, 'OK then, how can I buy this house with no money and still increase my income?'

After a short silence, the reply came:

"The amount of television you watch must have taught you by now that when it comes to trips and falls (sorry about the gym bag thing), 'where there's blame, there's a claim'. Now when it comes to buying something someone is selling, this is often true, 'Where there's pain, there's a gain'. It doesn't matter that the house is cheap, make it cheaper!"

Ding! A light bulb moment!

I decided to cash in on this roll we were on and asked my brain why my belly stuck out, but its mood had turned and was told, "because you eat too much, stupid!"

In the morning I called the agent and said I wanted to buy the place but needed another 5% off its market value.

She reminded me that it was already 10% under market value and that, if they knocked any more off, the vendors wouldn't have enough for their next place.

I embellished the truth (okay I lied) and told her that I already had a mortgage offer ready to go on the place, could complete before 'Junior' was born and slip smoothly like a shiny new link into this heaving chain.

She called back later to say that the person above them in the chain was flexible and could come down a bit, meaning they would take a bit less for theirs. I ended up with almost the 15% discount I wanted.

My legal team and I were now getting very used to working with each other; everyone else's legwork had already been done and we were able to get most of the details we needed from the original failed buyer. I picked up the keys four weeks later.

I had now decided that I would use my time more wisely and, although I could have saved a few quid by doing the painting myself, I got an odd-job guy in. Not only was he quicker than I would have been, he did a better job and I was able to cover the cost of his work by the fact that I was now able to let it sooner.

There was a hefty fee to change mortgage lenders so soon on the property, but the valuer had agreed with me that the property was conveniently worth 15% more than what I had paid for it. The lender also said that as long as I didn't go above 85% of the property's value they would give me a further advance. This meant that I was able to return the money I had begged and borrowed to the people and places it had come from to fund the initial deposit. The property was cash positive from day one and my total outlay to buy the place was just my legal fees and stamp duty, which I covered by way of my other places.

Further advances are sometimes called 'top-ups' or a term that banks and financial institutions use to encourage people to get themselves into debt: 'releasing equity'.

This romanticised term allows borrowers to feel like they are actually doing a good deed, a bit like they are letting a magnificent captive beast back onto the plains of the Serengeti. It gives them a clear conscience about the 'liability' debt they are plunging headlong into.

"Be free, Equity while I drive around in this brand new car that I will still be paying for fifteen years after I've scrapped it"

"Run wild, Equity as I get food poisoning on the two weeks holiday I didn't really enjoy that I'll spend ten years accruing interest on."

"Enjoy the vast grasslands, Equity as I'm working five years past retirement because I funded my daughter's wedding to some guy that wasn't good enough for her in the first place and who she later divorced. Be free, Equity, be free!"

I still find it hard to believe that it's glamorised by banks so as to seem almost noble, and advertised by celebrities we respect and feel like we almost know, but I suppose you can't really blame them. After all, a successful restaurant menu may show 'Hand carved British ham with poached free range eggs with a side dish of locally sourced chunky chips'. How successful would they be if they advertised 'Over-farmed dead pig, hacked up by some spotty drop-out with a septic nose ring, shoved on a plate with unfertilised chicken embryo and spuds too ugly to sell whole'? Which would *you* buy?

There is one very simple rule I have if I remortgage one of my rental properties.

- Any debt added to an income-producing asset must only be used to fund another income-producing asset.

In other words, it must go towards something that puts money in your pocket.

I've used the fruit (income) from my assets for many 'fun' things such as holidays, sports cars, motorbikes and much more but never the tree (the asset itself).

Rather than immediately buying a car, I used the money to buy a house. This house now funds the lease payments on my car, which depreciates by hundreds of pounds per month, as well as its high fuel costs, insurance, road tax and maintenance, etc.

If someone offers to sell you a liability, don't buy it! If you really want it, consider instead buying yourself an asset that will fund it.

If you're lucky enough to have a note of any kind in your pocket then get it out.

Have the Queen's head with her 'I'm so rich my face is on money' smirk facing you.

Now make two deliberate vertical folds down her face, one through each eye; then relax the note making sure the folds are still prominent. Hold the note with both hands at arm's length, as if parallel to a wall, and she'll still be smirking. Now tilt the top of the note forward a few degrees and have a look. This is what money taken from the tree (an asset) will probably bring you.

Next, close your eyes and, with the note at arm's length parallel to the wall again, tilt the top of the note back a few degrees. This is what money taken from the fruit (income from the asset) will probably bring you.

Good luck!

CHAPTER SEVEN

MOMENTUM

My next few properties were bought in a similar way to the last one: Find someone willing to sell with at least a 15% discount, put my own money in as a deposit and, on the day of completion, ask the lender to give it back to me.

As I perfected my sub prime, silver and gold buying strategy, it naturally clustered my houses together and, in the same street, I could have three or four properties.

With house shares, this made viewings much easier. I could show people a choice of room sizes on different floors, with different views and not get out of breath doing so.

I had gone back to my three storey four-beds and found a guy who needed to sell in a hurry. He had relocated with work to a town about 200 miles away and left his lodger behind. They'd had an agreement that this lodger and so-called friend would pay a token rent and act as 'caretaker'. All he had to do was let the other three rooms, collect the rent and send it on to his mate.

On paper this sounded like an easy win-win for both him and owner, but it all went wrong for the landlord very quickly. Not only did his lodger and so-called friend fail to pay any rent, even though he had a good job, he also decided that he preferred to live alone and made no effort to find any other paying guests for his friend.

After a while he got bored with that and moved some mates in, all on the house of course! One of these friends then stumbled across some post for the landlord and from that gathered enough information to open a bank account, take out some loans and credit cards, etc. all in the landlords name – nice bunch!

By this time, the landlord had had enough and just wanted rid of the place. He'd only had it a couple of years and was cursing the day he'd ever set eyes on it. The lodger and his mates had also started to trash the place a bit.

Houses in the area were selling very fast now. For first time buyers they were affordable. For investors they were well-priced and rented easily. The reason why this place wasn't selling was that whenever anyone viewed the house, it was in a right state, so much so that you couldn't get into some of the rooms for all the junk that was there. The guys living there were all part of the same rugby club and would huff, puff, snort, and walk around with chests out like a bunch of silverback gorillas, whenever anyone came to view, to protect the 'good thing' they were on.

Finally, and uncharacteristically for this area, the people living next door were very abrasive. It was one of the few council-owned houses left on the street and had been raided by the police a year or so before. The police had smashed the front door in and the council had then come round and boarded it up. The occupants refused to pay for the boarding-up as the police were well within their rights to have kicked it in. The council refused to fit a door as the occupants hadn't paid for the original boarding-up.

Thinking the council would fold, the family then wrote lots of messages to them on the boarded-up door for the world to see, some of which would have made a sailor blush!

This three-way stalemate continued for a couple of years. The occupants used the back door and neatly cut a letterbox in the boarding so the postman could still deliver their benefit cheques. The council took them to court and won, but the occupants had no money to pay them. They then proved that the house was a safety hazard as the only exit was through the kitchen and, with this being the most likely place for a fire to start, the council were eventually left with little choice but to replace the door or build them a fire exit. A door was cheaper and the council agreed to accept £1 a week from them until they were 107.

I didn't really want to buy a house that had neighbours like this and took a chance that they would evict these morons at a later date, as I got wind that they had upset a very senior councillor.

Surprised to see me for a second viewing of the property, the biggest silverback squared up to me on the stairs, saying that there was no way they were leaving and it was probably best that I didn't buy the place. At least that's what I thought he said, unburdened by the stress of having continents to structure into conversation; he seemed only to be able to speak in vowels. He had a scar running from the top of his ear to the middle of his head suggesting a brain repair, lobotomy, or some kind of experimentation.

I was two steps higher than him so we were about eye to eye. I decided that this put me in a winning position. If he hit me he would look like a bully and if I were able to push him down the stairs he would look even more foolish than he already did.

Nothing happened, so I smiled, said I would be in touch with the owner and squeezed politely past him.

I hit the owner with a very low offer which he declined; he knew why his place wasn't selling, but also knew my offer was insulting. We went back and forth for a while then reached a stalemate, so I walked away.

I never knew quite why, but something happened between the guys living there and the landlord and he then called the agent to say he wanted to accept my highest offer. I immediately reduced this offer by £5,000 and we struck a deal.

As soon as we had exchanged, I made sure that the agent and solicitor reminded the landlord that the place had to be void of human life and furniture prior to completion or he would be in breach of contract. Not wanting this to happen, he sprang into the action he should have done months earlier and, when I picked up the keys, the place was empty of mineral, animal and my friend the vegetable.

I cleaned it up, converted it to a five-bed, got the further advance to get my cash back out and found some great people to were all from the same country, on the same working at the same company. A good idea, I about three months after moving in, they all got ᵫade redundant and their visas were only renewed as students, so they couldn't work full time, and all fell behind on the rent.

I had to evict them, which wasn't pleasant for me, as I liked them all and, with the next lot, made sure that all my eggs weren't in one basket.

Incidentally, the next door family never did get evicted but the main troublemakers are now on a very long, government-funded holiday if you catch my drift.

I picked up another identical house a few streets away as the owner's wife had moved out and left him with a mortgage he couldn't afford and memories he didn't want. The price was even better than the last one even though the market was rising fast and my team, who were now like lightning, pushed things through quickly.

Conversions, further advance, good housemates, job done!

One of the agents I was now very friendly with, called to say that another one of these houses had just fallen through. The couple were emigrating in eight weeks and were very desperate to get a fast sell. They had reduced the price to reflect their situation and I got my team on the case straight away.

Then something very odd happened. Three weeks later and on the day of exchange, the vendor called to say that another buyer had offered them £10,000 more for the place. They were taking it and, as far as they were concerned, I could stick my offer, as they'd never really wanted to sell it to me in the first place.

I fully understood why they would take the higher offer; after all they were retiring as well as emigrating, so any extra money would be put to good use, but why had they made it so personal?

I had only met the couple once. The wife was lovely but the husband had made it very clear that he thought he was 'doing me a

74

favour' by letting me buy his house and that for some strange reason I should be grateful to him.

He didn't seem to like the fact that I wasn't.

I had also made the mistake of telling him my plans for the place without taking into consideration that it was still his family home and had been for the last twenty years. The place I was viewing as just 'bricks and sticks' was the house that he had worked hard to buy and raise his family in. I also got the impression from the agent that he was rude and patronising to anyone under fifty, so tried not to take things to heart.

I thought they were taking a big risk in accepting such a short notice offer, but told the agent to wish them luck and carried on looking for places.

Then a few weeks later and out of the blue, I got a call from the agent, who couldn't speak for the first minute as he was laughing so much, to say that the new buyer had failed to get a mortgage and with only two weeks left, flights booked, bags packed and many personal items already in transit they were in a right pickle.

Although I did laugh, I felt bad for them, but not so bad that I didn't lower my offer by several thousand pounds. It was very unlikely that another buyer could be found within their timescale and, with everything in place my end to exchange the next day, their hands were slightly tied.

The owner and I mutually avoided each other and didn't speak after that, although I do hope they are enjoying a very happy retirement.

One of the first guys to move into the house was Mike.

Like me, he was born in the UK and had a mixed heritage, but unlike me his father had gone home and he would spend time between there and the UK. Mike would drift between both countries for a while, never completely settling in either, but had eventually decided on the UK and got a job in a factory.

The media in his father's country idolised all that is western and with Mike being athletic, very good-looking and light-skinned in a sort of 'diet black' kind of way, he became a successful model and even did some television work. He was very modest and almost shy; he'd had bad experiences with landlords before and I could see he was uncomfortable around me. Initially, I was worried that he had something to hide, and maybe he did, but nothing ever surfaced.

I was still reading a couple of books a month on investment, so we agreed to meet in a coffee shop to sort out the deposit and contracts. He brought his mum with him who seemed very respectable. I had watched him take the cash out from the hole-in-the-wall opposite so knew he wasn't 'borrowing' the deposit.

Generally, it's a good idea to find out where someone is getting their deposit from as, not only does it gauge their ability to save and budget, it gives you an idea of how much the money means to them. Like a deposit on a house, if there was some pain involved in making that money then, in most cases, people will do all they can to get it back.

Parents will quite often spend money like water on deposits for a 'problem' they don't want at home but still want to know is safe. Meeting parents is also a very good indicator when selecting people and I've found it's very useful to casually interview them as much as their offspring. Junior could be primed with all the questions you might ask to subtly catch them out, but quite often the parents won't be. Mum and dads' car will quite often give you an idea of their upbringing.

I could tell that Mike's mum was a real grafter and had worked hard to bring her family up, so I had no qualms in letting Mike have a room.

With every girl in the coffee shop blushing slightly and fanning herself, I took Mike's deposit, we signed the paperwork and I gave him the keys. He moved into one of my best house shares and fitted in very well. He was clean, tidy, quiet and incredibly polite.

He was still nervous around me for some reason although

getting better, but would occasionally tell the other guys in the house that if they ever wanted him to leave, then all they had to do was tell him and he would go. No one knew why he would say this as he was very well-liked and a real asset to the house. I was also pleased to find out from another sharer that he was going to night classes to improve his education and help further his career. I can honestly say that I only had praise for Mike and have rarely come across a more popular character.

After he had been there a year or so, I got a call from one of his housemates asking me for access to his room. Andrew wanted to go in there to take out a couple of 'lad mags' he had loaned him.

I was chin deep in paperwork when Andrew called and I told him that I could only go into Mike's room with his permission, unless I had given him sufficient notice or there was an emergency. I couldn't really see the point of the call. He would just have to wait until he saw Mike or just bloody ring him. Paperwork is something I hate doing and am not very good at. One of the things the investment books hadn't told me was just how much there was going to be as my portfolio grew.

There was a short silence and Andrew said quietly, "I can't wait to see Mike."

"Where are you going then?" was my short reply.

There was another silence before Andrew said, "I'm not going anywhere... Mike is dead."

In a gut-wrenching paradigm shift, my mountain of paperwork suddenly paled into insignificance.

I hoped for a punch line or to find out he was joking, but it didn't come.

Mike had committed suicide a few hours before.

I found out from his housemates that he had recently run into some difficulty and had expressed some fears for his safety. He had met a girl at work; a group of lads had objected to this and had been giving him a hard time. I'm not sure how much of a hard time but he had felt the need to take up self-defence classes and would rarely go out socially in the weeks leading up to his death. In true Mike fashion and not wanting to put anyone out, he had driven to a remote place to end his life.

I can't even start to comprehend what sort of pain he must have been going through to drive him to this, but the housemates and I were all reduced to tears over it on several occasions.

Andrew knew that Mike's family were coming to collect his personal items and they had previously made a drunken pact that they would remove anything they didn't want their mums to see if anything ever happened to one of them. Andrew had taken this as light-hearted banter. I don't know what Mike's thoughts had been at the time.

His housemates did Mike, themselves and me proud on the lead up to the funeral. They made themselves available for Mike's family, organised a wreath, etc. And all but one took a day off for the funeral.

There was a very good turnout and I was glad to be able to pass on my condolences, reminisce and share the loss caused by Mike's early departure.

As a landlord, I have great respect for the people I'm lucky enough to have renting from me and, although I didn't show it, was once again brought to tears. This time not by Mike's death, but by what his housemates had achieved together.

CHAPTER EIGHT

FINDING AND SELECTING SHARERS

For the first few years after becoming the House Share Hero, I would constantly experience the following imbalance:

20% OF THE PEOPLE RENTING FROM ME TAKE UP 80% OF MY TIME.

At the time, I didn't know why this was happening; I just knew that it was. I'd never even heard of 'Prato's rule' but was sure getting hammered by it.

Some were late payers; some were disruptive or inconsiderate to others. Some had standards so high that they were always asking for unnecessary maintenance or felt the need to keep you updated on every finite detail of what was happening around them. Conversely, some had standards that were so low that others wanted to update me on what *they* were up to.

I've learnt some effective techniques and implemented some first class systems to pretty much eliminate these problems from my business. I will unfold some of these in the next few chapters.

My house shares are in solid working class, middle class and affluent areas, with many of these being 'over supplied' with house shares, However, I have higher occupancy rates than other landlords as well as a higher standard of person renting from me.

Coincidentally, I also choose each of my customers personally.

I've had thousands of people pass through my houses over the years but until I learned how to apply very simple but extremely effective techniques for marketing, management and systemisation, as well as the people I have told you about so far, I've had those who use dish cloths and tea towels for toilet paper and then put them back. I've had calls in the evening asking me to remove spiders from properties. I've had an irate call at midnight from a sharer who had come home to find out that one of his housemates had eaten his yoghurt. I've rented to a couple of newly-weds who fell out and the husband was stabbed by the wife. I've had sharers get beaten up, beat each other up, get arrested and even deported. They've gotten fellow housemates pregnant on more than one occasion and each time it's ended in tears. I've entered properties to find things missing, damaged and people growing cannabis, or committing fraud. In one incident, I found one of my sharers only hours from death and in urgent need of medical attention.

I've had people try to avoid, blackmail, lie to me, and threaten me. I've lost money, time and sleep over the years, all through doing things the same way that other landlords were doing things.

Through trial, error, self education and necessity, my life is now pretty easy.

Like most house share landlords, I was playing the 'short game' and was at high risk of burn-out after a few years.

I constantly see landlords come in to multi-letting, applying the same techniques as they would for single lets, or worse still, none at all and packing it in after just a few months or years vowing never to go back into the dark murky waters of multi-lets.

If you're red lining your stress, skill and stamina levels in anything you do, and especially as a house share landlord, you're likely to crash and burn.

If you look at the opposition of the likes of Roger Federer, Muhammad Ali and Usain Bolt when they are/were in their peak, for instance, you will see someone red lining just to stay in the game whilst their brilliant foe is still in second gear. And when the opposition does raise their game, they are swiftly and effectively put in their place.

When you can run a better business than your competitors without leaving first or second gear, then your opportunities are limitless.

What most books, television shows and so-called 'property experts' won't tell you is that buying the houses is by far the easiest part of making money with property. The real heartbeat of your empire *is* your customer.

Finding the right people to live in your houses.

As mentioned, I now have great systems in place for finding, selecting, looking after and retaining the people who live in my houses. I'm pleased to say that my business runs very well, provides me with a great income and should also provide a good investment for, not only my retirement, but also my children's future.

<u>Finding Sharers:</u>

When it comes to finding the right candidates for my properties, I use very simple, tried and tested techniques.

The easiest way to find great sharers in average areas and up is via the Internet.

Most people these days have access to a computer and, as a landlord, sites, such as, *Easyroommate.co.uk*, *Gumtree.co.uk* and *Spareroom.co.uk* are free or cheap to advertise on and accessible to more people than the local paper. This is especially true for people coming into the UK who are searching for a place before they get here. A good percentage of my professional sharers come to me this way and what I spend in a year here is less than what I would spend a month on printed ads. I will also apply other techniques to get to these people before they even post an ad on the internet as, although being better than your competition is great, not having any competition is even better!

Advertising in the local paper is expensive and outdated, but I still find it useful for finding good people to live in more working class areas. They are more likely to be familiar with looking for jobs and cars in this fashion, so looking for housing this way is quite often their obvious choice, although this is slowly shifting. I find the majority of my sharers and single unit renters for working class areas this way.

I also make sure I'm known as a landlord who can help people. With less than 10% of the people who contact me ending up in one of my places, most of the people I turn down will be suitable for other landlords I know. It might just be that they don't fit the demographic I'm looking for, or in most cases I'm full. Where I can't help, I will always pass them over to another landlord who can, or will give them some other pointers. As my marketing is so effective, the other landlords I work with are very happy to pay me a referral fee for the people I pass their way that I can't help, and I'm very happy to get paid for the people I turn down! Now there's a real win – win!

This has four main benefits: My company is known locally to be able to find places for most people. Almost all calls end on a positive note with either me helping someone find a place or giving them a good opportunity to find someone who can. This in turn means that people will often contact my company first as it's seen as an easy route to finding somewhere to live.

The second benefit is that I know what's happening in my local market; I know the landlords who are full and the ones looking for people. I know the landlords who look after their customers and the ones who only care about their rent. I know those who struggle and those who do well. I know what other landlords charge and what they offer for this price.

When a landlord's business collapsed recently and his houses were repossessed, most of the dozen or so of his customers came to me for somewhere to live. Even though I wasn't actively advertising and was full at the time, we were able to find some very good places for them.

It's vital that you know who your competition is and what they are doing. You can achieve much more by working with them than by working against them. It can also be very lonely being a landlord, so having a good community around you is very important. House Share Heroes are people too!

The third benefit is that when I have a unit coming up, I can 'put the word out'. I would say that I give far more than I receive, but this is still another good way of finding people.

Finally, and very importantly, when any of us are getting rid of a 'bad un' or we know one is looking for a place, we discreetly let each other know. Nearly every landlord I work with has saved another some heartache by letting him or her know what 'nutters' are on the lookout!

We all have the name 'Ignore' or 'Don't pick up' programmed in our phones so when the people we don't want do call, we don't even have to speak to them!

As I've mentioned, I'm lucky to have fantastic people renting from me. For that reason I offer them cash incentives to recommend their friends, family and work colleagues to also rent from me, as good people will generally work and socialise with like-minded ones.

I like to think they would recommend me anyway, but a cash incentive perhaps pushes things closer to the front of their minds if they come across or overhear that someone is looking for a place.

Selecting the best people:

Selecting the best people for your places is fundamental to the success of your property business, whether you have one house or one hundred houses, you are running a business, and the ability to choose good people is essential. Good companies need good people, good shops need good products and good landlords need good customers; it really is that simple.

All the bad experiences I have had so far have been or were during my own learning curve and, even now, I have a few customers who have been with me for years who, to be completely fair to them, don't cause me any problems, but they would fail my de-selection process if they contacted me today. It's a skill that constantly needs honing and, like an athlete, or someone at the top of their game, you need to work on this skill all the time. A boxer, who hasn't been in the ring for a while, still knows exactly what he has to do, but when he tries to do it, he has 'ring rust'. His timing is off. Only when he starts doing the things that he already knows, over and over again, will his timing and accuracy return. As a landlord, you won't lose your fights in the ring; you would have already lost them in the gym beforehand. When I follow my own simple systems for finding sharers, it's easy; when I deviate from what works, I lose efficiency and problems move in. You may have a better house than mine, in a better street, but more people will be getting in touch with me than with you because I practise my skills daily.

A lot of my advertising is automated or requires just a click of a button to reach thousands of people and my website is open 24/7. This means I get an oversupply of enquiries from people looking for places. Even if I'm full, I will have an informal chat with them and, at the same time, I will be casually and subtly interviewing them. If I'm full but think they are suitable, but they need a place right now, I will not only make sure the next landlord they speak to will be one that will be able to help them, but my 'marketing magnet' will capture their details and pop them in my little sales funnel to draw them to me at a later date.

Rental properties and especially house shares are also like your children. Most people will wish you good health and happiness for them but no one will ever truly love them like you do. Think of a letting agent as their nursery nurse who will look after them to some degree but, like your friends, when your train does leave for

Crapville, all they will do is wish you well.

I recently got a call from a landlord to say that he'd had a fire in one of his houses. This landlord is a fantastic guy and I have the utmost respect for him, his business, his attitude and his family. He was devastated and I felt terrible for him, as it couldn't have happened to a nicer guy. When my wife and I sat down for dinner that evening, she noticed that I was down and I told her what had happened to my friend. She too was genuinely sad for him. We hoped things would be OK for him and as I started my dinner the next thing to pop into my mind was: Bloody hell! This steak is delicious!

My friend was on *his* train and I had just started waving.

Make sure you have the skills, knowledge and capability to manage your houses yourself – especially house shares. Even if you use an agent to do it, you must be talking to them on the same level. Only then will you know when they are doing a good or bad job and they will respect you more as a landlord because of this. If they are going to take liberties, it will be with the guy that's never stepped into their arena before. You may be carrying a few pounds and your Hero costume might be praying you don't bend over, but the agents will know not to mess you about.

Know and understand the skills you need to be successful, even if you're not directly involved day to day. If two identical people with two identical cars take them to a garage for repair and one says, "I don't even know where the petrol goes", whilst the other says "I used to own three garages just like this". Who do you think will get the lowest bill?

Since 1997, I've never credit-checked a sharer, as I would estimate that at least half to two-thirds would not pass, but my arrears generally only run at about 1 or 2% of my receivable rent and arrears that aren't agreed beforehand, however, are even less than this. I also rarely rely on referencing as, if you asked a room full of landlords if they would give a bad person a good reference to get rid of them, you will see a lot of red faces! If you want a reference, get it from the landlord before their current one for a truthful one.

Before meeting people to show them properties, I generally only ask five questions which are:

1. What are they looking for?
2. Where are they looking?
3. Why are they looking?
4. Where do they work?
5. When are they looking to move?

The first open question allows me to listen to them 'just talk'. Everyone has a criterion or wish list, and those who really don't care where they live should be probed further and generally avoided. It's also the time to check out their attitude, what words they are using and if they are 'over familiar' or 'odd balls'. I will generally know after they have finished answering this question whether I want to ask them any more. Anyone who starts off by saying "What it is, is. . ." will always be dismissed as the next words out of their mouths wont be "I have a very good job, get on well with people and am extremely reliable."

And if you feel you want to ask "Yah get meh?" then I'm sorry to say that I don't.

Finally, and unless you're a high ranking Native American who employs a sibling, avoid those who call you: 'Chief', 'Boss' or 'Bruv'!

If I'm happy then I will find out where they are looking. This lets me gauge how much they have really thought this through and, if I haven't got any places in that area, I can get a feel as to how flexible they are and the type of neighbourhood they're looking for. It may even transpire that I offer them something across town with the first option on a place in their chosen area as soon as it comes up.

Why they are looking is a hard question to ask, as sometimes the answers can be quite personal. It might be as straightforward as, they are new to the area, but occasionally it can be quite emotive like divorce or separation. I've had plenty of people burst into tears on me after asking this one. I'm looking for genuine reasons here and you will be surprised to find people actually saying things like:

"I've just got out of prison", "The wife has kicked me out for beating her up again" and my very favourite, "My landlord is evicting me!"

After this question I won't talk straight away. The reason for this is that if you're quiet, the person you're talking to will feel compelled to say something else. It's as if you're silently nudging them to say that they haven't answered the question properly or you're expecting more. Initially it's hard to do this, but it does pay off. A second of 'dead' airtime with someone you don't know very well will seem like a minute to them and, if they are going to trip up or reveal too much, which they often will, then this is one of the times they will do it.

The answer: "I've just got a new job in the area" followed by nothing from you might then provoke, "Because I was sacked from my last one".

Try this next time you're talking to someone and you will see how well it works. Don't try it with someone who adores you, as they will just be happy listening to the sound of your breathing!

Where they work is another great indicator of how good a renter they will be. Responsible people generally get responsible jobs, etc. and if your local knowledge is good enough you may even know what the company they work for is like and what type of people they employ. You may even have a contact there.

If you think they are lying or are not sure of your own judgment of people, ask to see their job offer if they are just starting, or their most recent pay slip and find out which department they work in and ring up before you even agree to meet them.

Don't ask: "Does Fred Smith work here?" as you will normally get quoted sections of the data protection act and may slip into a coma. Just ask cheerfully, "Hi, is Fred Smith in today?"

The answers you want are, "Yes", "No, it's his day off" or "He's on a course". You don't want to hear things like, "No, we've sacked him", "never heard of him" or my personal favourite, "Are you calling from the bailiffs again?"

Finally, by finding out when they are looking to move, you can best match them to the places you have available or coming up. You don't want to find the perfect person for an empty unit only for them to drop the bombshell that they want to move in three months time! It happens. Also if they need something "Like yesterday" then be cautious and probe further. Are they really that disorganised or unlucky, or is there more to their story? Quite often these are the 'Monday morningers' who have been kicked out over the weekend but will be back in love and not wanting to move after you have spent an afternoon showing them places.

From the people who contact me for rental places, only about 20-30% will get to see a place. Typically, the figures will look like this for every ten people who get in touch:

- Two will be dismissed as unsuitable within the first twenty to thirty seconds and offered practical advice.
- Four will be dismissed as unsuitable during the five questions, or may be looking for something we can't offer and given the numbers of someone who can help.
- Four will be deemed suitable for a property and offered a viewing.
- One will have found a place or changed his/her mind.
- Three of them will view somewhere and, in most cases, offered a place.
- One or two of them will take it.

As you can see, using the five questions will help whittle your applicants down nicely and help you to use your time effectively.

The way I 'find' and 'select' my sharers is one of the main reasons why I work only a few hours a day, don't work Fridays,

Saturdays or Sundays and can take time off when I choose and love what I do.

I didn't really get any long term enjoyment from any of the jobs I once had and very rarely meet people who can honestly put their hand on their heart and say that they love their jobs.

I know people who don't see their families as much as they would like to, who work longer and longer hours, never realising that their hourly rate after promotion was the same as or less than before. I know people who work seventy to eighty hour weeks for free, for someone else, who are waiting for the time when things quieten down so they can get the time back. I have friends who are very cash rich and, at the same time, live in time poverty. I know people who are living hand-to-mouth wondering how they are going to pay the mortgage each month, or if their maxed-out credit card will be accepted for the food shopping. I have friends that will spend half our time together telling me about the latest rounds of redundancies at their workplace and the other half telling me that what I do lacks security.

I'm pleased to say that I don't have any of those problems any more and will fight tooth and nail never to acquire them in the future!

CHAPTER NINE

MINDING YOUR OWN BUSINESS

Managing Yourself:

'Managing yourself' might seem like a strange statement, but once I had established that time was my biggest asset and not money, it was imperative that I made sure I wasn't making the same two biggest mistakes as most landlords did.

The first, and what I feel is a cardinal sin in having customers, is ignoring them. Too many landlords either avoid dealing with the problems of their sharers or continually over-promise and under-deliver. When the questions get hard, the landlord's availability suddenly diminishes.

I also know landlords who are more like bullies and some that are so soft they get constantly walked over.

As with most things in life, a firm, fair approach will serve you well and although this may sound like a cliché, your goal should be to gain respect rather than camaraderie. If they like you too, then that's a bonus.

In my business it's often hard saying 'no' to someone's request, but if I feel it's the right thing to do then I will. The worst thing you can do is leave people hanging on while you dilly-dally, make promises you can't deliver or, worse still, just go silent on them.

The second thing I do my utmost to avoid is 'majoring in minors'. In most professions you can spend your days running around dealing with minute problems that really don't need solving, or that someone else, better suited to the problem, could have dealt with. Problems are like little weights on a chain around your neck. We all have them, but if you let them, people will be constantly trying to add links to yours. This is never truer than if you are a landlord. It is therefore vital that you empower people to deal with their own problems.

Concentrate on 'time savers' and not 'time thieves'.

Here are some examples of what I used to do and what I do now:

Query:

"The wheelie bin has been stolen"

Time thief:

"Ill order new a one". Spend twenty minutes on hold only to find out that the bin I want replaced is supplied by a different department. Spend another twenty minutes on hold only to get asked a load of questions about where the bin was placed when it went, was it put out correctly and have I checked the neighbours. Call the person back to get the answers but she's working and can't talk in her break. Finally get the information and spend twenty minutes on the phone to the council again before they agree to send another bin out. Call the sharer back to advise that a new rubbish bin is on its way, only to be informed that it was the recycling bin that was taken.

Time saver:

"I'm sorry to hear that. Here's the number for the council; if you call them they will send you a new one."

Query:

Tina calls to say, "Frank isn't cutting the grass when it's his turn."

Time thief:

Chase Frank, only to be told that it's not his turn, it's Ian's and that Tina and her boyfriend have been keeping him awake with their drunken lovemaking. Call Ian who says he thought it was Frank's turn and Frank has been leaving the front door unlocked.

Call Tina who is embarrassed and says she hasn't even got a boyfriend. Call Frank to say the others say it's his turn and ask why he's leaving the front door unlocked, only to be told that he cut the grass last time and it's David who isn't locking the front door.

Time saver:

Thank Tina for bringing this to our attention and advise that she should speak to the other housemates to draw up a rota, as they are all equally liable and, if the grass gets too long to cut, our gardener has a minimum charge of £60 to come out and do it for them. In addition to this, remind them that they have signed an agreement to say that they are all jointly and severely liable for any loss or damage to shared areas and should decide if keeping the front door locked is a good idea in light of this.

Query:

"The washing machine door is broken"

Time Consumer:

Go the property; find out the make and model of the machine. Come back home and order a new hinge. When the part comes, go back to the house and realise that to take the door apart to fit the new hinge requires a special tool that I don't have. Find the tool in the third DIY shop visit. Go back to the house and, with two sharers standing over me, take the door apart, lose a screw under the fridge, get angry and lose my temper with the door. Get my jeans dirty and then find out that the door won't close as I got one of the digits wrong on the model number. Swear profusely.

Time Saver:

Get a (wo)man in.

As mentioned, these days I don't get most of the problems and issues that other landlords do, and the reason for this is that nearly all of my customers pay their rent on time every month, are clean and tidy, stay longer than they planned to, get along with each other and are a pleasure to have living in my houses.

The few and far between problems I *do* get are made up of the people who 'only just' got a place as I bent or broke my own rules or, for some reason, have fallen on hard times.

I will be proactive with these guys and make sure that we are both crystal clear on what I expect from them. In other words, I 'look after' the majority and 'manage' the minority.

Rent problems

If someone is having problems with their rent, we agree on a written payment plan. I explain clearly that I will do all I can to help people who 'can't' pay their rent and will work with them until they are back on their feet. We agree timescales for bringing things back on track, what dates they will pay and the times they will call me or email me with updates of their situation. Where possible, I will let them decide on the amount and frequency and, if I think they have overestimated the speed at which they can eliminate their arrears, I will suggest a lower amount to pay off arrears over a longer period. My landlord software and diary on my mobile phone is to remind me of what we have agreed and to inform me immediately if they have deviated from this. If someone was due to call me at 10am, I will politely chase him or her at 10:02am.

Quite often, inconsistent payers will want credit from you when they pay correctly, and say things like:

"My last two rent payments were on time, so why are you on my back about this one?"

So far I have resisted my natural urge to say, "It's supposed to be on time you low expectation idiot!" and just remind them of their contractual obligation. These are generally the types who will also want credit for 'never going to prison' or 'looking after their kids' and will probably find that they are more suited to another landlord.

I make it clear that if they stick to the payment plan we have agreed, then their tenancy will be safe, and that I fully understand that sometimes people 'can't pay'. I make sure they know how grateful I am that they have told me in advance. As they breathe a sigh of relief, I take the opportunity to tell them about another category of people I have no time for, who are the 'won't pays'. I quantify this to them by making sure we both understand that I consider those to be people who don't pay their rent without prior agreement, or don't stick to agreed payment plans and call me with updates on or before the time agreed. I tell them that I take these actions personally and that I'm glad they're not one of these people. I tell them that in all my years of being a landlord, I have always had more time, resources, expertise and experience in chasing 'won't pays' than they have had in avoiding me and that I will do (legally) all it takes to recover monies owed.

I end the conversation by saying that I'm sure this won't happen in their case and I look forward to talking to them shortly.

Behaviour problems

In nearly all the cases of behaviour problems, you will find that it's just down to a misunderstanding of some kind. It might be that the person didn't realise that parking on the front lawn was unacceptable or that when it's hot they can't take your sofas out into the garden. They might not have remembered that their contract says in three places, and you have already told them once, that they can't keep a pet or smoke in the property, but they have still gone out and bought an ex-circus chimp with a 20-a-day habit.

Generally, one gentle reminder will resolve most behaviour problems.

If it does, great, but if it doesn't, then don't waste too much more time with them. If they couldn't give a monkey's (excuse the pun) when you ask them once, then they are unlikely to take notice when you ask them again.

I make it clear that I'm not their boss, friend, or parent and it's entirely up to them how they respond to my request. I say all of this politely and ensure that they realise the ball is in their court. They will either shape up, ship out or I will ship them out.

In house shares I will also ensure that the other housemates know I am taking their complaints very seriously and explain that, although the law dictates that solving some problems may take a few weeks or months, it's always at the forefront of my activities.

This is important as the other housemates are living with this problem and will quite often 'unify' to resolve things with much more speed and efficiency than I can.

Before I perfected the 'five questions' and had learned how to 'manage myself', I went through the experience of meeting Gerald. He had viewed a couple of my properties; he was a middle-aged man who was accompanied by his wife. They were splitting up and she was helping him find a place. What a lovely lady, I thought to myself . . . sigh.

Gerald missed out on a couple of places, as people who viewed them around the same time paid the deposits there and then. There were also a couple of houses where I didn't think he would fit in with the other housemates for various reasons, mainly down to the fact that he was around twenty years older than most of my other sharers.

He was a nice, jolly guy and I didn't want him to lose out on a place, so I made sure that he got the next suitable room that was available. He reminded me of someone's 'friendly dad'.

Gerald's wife paid the deposit for him and, as I told her that Gerald's new place was now confirmed, her eyes filled with tears and she immediately looked ten years younger. 'That's nice!' I thought.

When Gerald turned up to move in, he looked smart and was his normally friendly self and I felt comfortable giving him the keys.

Things went well for the first three months. The local kids loved him; he was always clean, tidy and respectable and got on well with his housemates. Whenever I saw him, it was a pleasure.

What I didn't know about was Gerald's deeply hidden secret and even deeper rooted addiction. He wasn't a cowboy, but the times I had met him, I had no way of knowing that he had been securely bolted to a wagon by his long-suffering family!

For the twenty years before I had met Gerald, alcoholism had been his kryptonite. He would steal, lie and cheat to get hold of his 'poison' and had learned to hide this addiction from almost everyone. Bizarrely, he would never admit to it either. On a few occasions I would find Gerald passed out, surrounded by empty cans and bottles and the next day he would say he had been ill or asleep. The booze was never his and he hardly drank at all if he was honest.

I'm no psychologist and will freely admit to know hardly anything about addiction. One thing I do know, however, is that unless you can see or admit to yourself that you have a problem, any fixes you can make will be only temporary at best.

The doctors, counsellors and Gerald's beleaguered family had been trying for two decades to work from the outside in to help him but with minimal results. They had papered over his cracks long enough to make a good impression and then pointed him in my direction. His last dry spell had been during the times I'd met him and, for a short while, after moving in to one of my houses.

With no one there to tell him to take his tablets, go to the meetings and check his shopping, his resolve had weakened and he eventually started to fall off the wagon. It had been a gradual, well-hidden process but Gerald's wagon was now just a puff of dust on the horizon of his alcoholic wilderness.

His family had dreaded that this would happen and knew they were just shifting this problem my way. Did I blame them? No. On the one hand I wished I'd never met them, but they had taken Gerald as far as they could. They had lived with him and had their lives marred by his addiction and, unlike Gerald, they could now admit they were at rock bottom. They had stayed with him as long as they could on his journey but couldn't go any further and were spent. Their tanks were too empty and their hearts too heavy keep going. It wasn't personal; it was just the status quo.

I first noticed Gerald's problem when he agreed to put some furniture together for me. He had been laid-off from work and this would keep him busy for a day or two and help him pay back some of the arrears he was starting to build up.

I picked him up at 8.am on the morning he was due to start the job and noticed a faint smell of alcohol. Surely it was too early to have had a drink; I assumed it was from the night before. It was a month or so since I had last seen him and he looked a bit ropey. His hair was long; he hadn't shaved and had lost at least a stone in weight.

Apart from that he seemed in good form and I showed him what I wanted doing. He told me that flat packs were a doddle and to leave him to it; said he used to build diesel engines for a living so this would be a piece of cake.

About an hour later I popped back to the house to drop off some more items, as Gerald had said that what I'd left would keep him going for a short while. I found him face down on the floor.

He had opened all the boxes at once and built some kind of 'Frankendrobe' that stood swaying in the middle of the room. There was no sign of any alcohol but the smell from him had gotten worse so I assumed he had collapsed.

I gave him a quick shake; he came to with a start, mumbled something about being sorry and half walked, half crawled out of the front door and off into the distance.

When I caught up with him a few days later, he told me he'd had a virus and a bad reaction to the medication?

I wasn't so sure.

As the weeks went on, the council agreed to pay Gerald's housing benefit but, because he was never in a fit state to go and see them, or answer the door when they called, he was now nearly three months behind with his rent. I decided that I had no choice but to evict him and went to the house to serve him notice.

The house was immaculate as always: another trick he had learned was to localise the devastation, but what greeted me in his room was beyond belief.

When he answered his door I was immediately overwhelmed with the smell of human excrement and taken further aback by a swarm of bluebottles flying past me.

Not only was Gerald covered in a thin layer of his own waste; nearly everything in his room was too. The door, the walls, the carpets... His mattress was soaked through to the point where it was dripping onto the floor below.

As he hadn't been eating and only consuming alcohol, his faeces were mostly composed of a thin liquid.

There were piles of soiled underwear stacked in a corner of the bedroom, and rather than go to the bathroom, which was next door. He had put a towel on the armchair I had provided him with, and was using that as some kind of commode.

Once again Gerald put this down to an illness.

As the weeks went on to his pending eviction, I kept in close contact with his family and between us we checked in on him daily.

He seemed to be deteriorating hourly and wouldn't open the door for the doctor. At the time I was upgrading some other properties and Gerald was getting through the mattresses from these houses at a rate of one a week. As much as I wanted him out, I also wanted to give the guy some dignity.

The other housemates still didn't know how bad the problem was, as it was completely isolated to his room. The rest of the house was still spotless and, luckily, the heavy fire door on his bedroom was creating a good barrier for the smells.

The last time I saw Gerald, he was unconscious. I knew he was in and his contract stated that I was within my rights to enter his room, with his consent, or in an emergency. For some reason, I instinctively knew that the latter was very relevant at that point, so I took a deep breath, put a cloth over my nose and mouth and opened the door.

Gerald looked completely lifeless and – more worrying – colourless. I shouted, poked him and tried to get him to come round. His body was cold and stiff so I decided he was either dead or close to it. He then stirred slightly, which was a relief, not only because this meant he was still alive, but also I couldn't have faced giving him mouth-to-mouth.

I called for an ambulance first and then his son.

Gerald was so ill that he stayed in hospital for nearly three months. He spent the first two weeks not knowing who he was, and the next two in a very serious state of withdrawal; often fighting with the hospital staff and his family who visited every day. He was given various treatments to help him on his recovery, and his family and I worked closely with the local housing officer. When he was well enough, he was moved into a housing complex where he could have independence but also be watched over.

About a week after Gerald was released, he called me to say 'thanks' for calling the ambulance. It was great talking to the 'old Gerald' again and I asked him how he was.

He told me he was much better now and ready to get on with his life. We both knew what had happened to him and we each knew that the other knew.

Gerald was insistent that he'd just had another mystery 'virus' but was fine now. He said he would stay in touch and promised to pay me every penny of the rent he owed me.

That was in 2004 and I didn't hear from him again for six years, and then something very strange happened.

For a long time after Gerald moved out, I crossed paths occasionally with members of his family every now and again, but my ever-hopeful smiles were always met with sad, shaking heads.

Then, around the start of 2010, I started getting phone calls from some really good applicants who, although had never heard of my company or received any of my marketing, wanted to live in my houses and would even wait until I had something available, if I was full or live in one of my places on the opposite side of town to where they wanted to be and perhaps face a long bus ride until I had something closer to their work.

They were all very clean, tidy and reliable care workers and it took me a little while to figure out they all had one thing in common – GERALD!

Although still plagued by alcoholism, Gerald is now lucky enough to be living in sheltered accommodation. This means that he can be semi independent and at the same time kept safe.

I haven't spoken to Gerald, but I hear from his care workers that he's just about ok and that he shows all of the agency care workers that look after him a tatty old business card that he keeps in his wallet and tells them:

"If you want a great landlord, call this guy!"

Since then, we've exchanged regards through his care workers and I've sent him some new business cards.

I don't know how many years, months or weeks Gerald has left, but I hope, one day, he will be able to make the most of them.

CHAPTER TEN

A STITCH IN TIME

About the time I'd decided that a 'day's work for a day's pay' was actually quite time-consuming, the bank was also starting to insist that my office was in reality *their* office and that they would like me to concentrate on *their* business while I was in it and not my own.

It was time to think about leaving. By this time, I was so far off the bottom of the sales leagues that they weren't just spelling my name incorrectly; sometimes they didn't include me at all. They didn't give me too much hassle about this for nearly a year, as I was now tucked away in a little branch, so was well off the radar. I wasn't really causing any problems either and had been a very good seller for them in the past. They also had plenty of other fish to fry before finally getting round to me.

The situation finally came to a head when they sent the area manager to see me. I had a great deal of respect for her as she had nurtured and helped my career since I'd met her on my first day at the bank. She was kind-hearted and very good at her job and had progressed through the ranks at a good pace.

It was now time for her to get tough and tell me to pull my finger out or pack my stuff. We had a long discussion about how they would be monitoring me if I stayed, and it became clear that their plan was to 'micro manage' me for a couple of months, to force me to sink or swim. It was slightly farcical as, even if I did want to do well, I would be spending so much time filling in compliance forms that I would have no time to see customers so would fail anyway! I was on the wrong end of some pretty clever and completely justified tactics from the bank.

As a manager, and member of the union, I was in a position to have up to a year off with full pay if I became ill. There were a few people taking full advantage of this and one manager would even come back to work for four weeks and one day every year to reinstate this benefit before taking another year off, but it wasn't really my style. We both knew that I was more than capable of being at the top of the table again and that, at the same time, no longer had any fire left in my belly to make it happen. When people used to come in for a loan for a Ford or a Vauxhall, I would remind them how hard they worked and talk them up to a BMW or Mercedes. These days I was advising them to repair their old car and open a cash ISA instead.

I'd been working for three days a week in my last year at the bank. My bills were now being covered by my rental properties and had been for the last eighteen months (coincidently the same time that my sales started to fall away). I could have easily quit a year before but didn't have the bottle; I was enjoying the essentially 'free money' I was getting. Penny gave me the push I needed which I'm hugely grateful for and, I'm pleased to say, I haven't looked back and much prefer to be a customer than an employee.

For the first six months after I quit the bank, I would generally finish running my house shares, would have had lunch and a work out about 1 or 2pm.

I'd find a comfy seat in a local coffee house and sit, read and drink coffee. I did this pretty much every weekday. I would read every property, investment and self-help book I could find, as well as listening to a dozen or so audio courses. The bank was a couple of doors down the road and I would cheerfully wave to my old work mates as they walked by. Most would wave back, but occasionally a couple seemed to mouth the words 'Banker' to me, which seemed odd, but perhaps they didn't know I'd left. To them it must have seemed like I was extremely lazy but, in reality, the coffee shop window was my new classroom. There is no secret or quick fix to gain understanding about what I was doing; I was relentlessly driving my self study, self learning and self development. My current portfolio was also affording me the practical skills I needed and I was repeating this procedure every day, over and over again: training my mind, learning my skills, challenging my beliefs and searching for gold.

After a while I kept striking gold again and again. It might have been in an entire CD course or just one line in a book, but the more I prospected, the more I found. So much so, that I was struggling to keep up with it.

The reticular activation system buried deep inside my brain, unbeknownst to me was becoming ever increasingly drawn to any scrap of information that would help me become a better landlord. This in turn was increasing my income, which gave me more time to locate, analyse and create property deals and grow my portfolio. It was becoming self-perpetuating and, I must say, slightly addictive (but that might have been the coffee).

What was happening to me is more commonly known as 'The law of attraction'.

If you have ever been pregnant or know someone close to you that has, it suddenly seems that half the world is also pregnant. The same is true if you buy a new car; you become aware of how many people also have the same, or a similar car. The reason for this is that you are being drawn to the things you are focusing on. This is a very powerful tool and can work in ways that you would find hard to believe.

It can also be extremely negative. If you walk round all day thinking, "I must not bump my head, I must not bump my head" then guess what? Although you don't want to, you are actually focusing on 'bumping your head'!

The Secret by Rhonda Byrne explains how the laws of attraction work, more clearly than I ever could and I recommend that you study the book, audio course and DVD. Although they all have the same message, I found the DVD and audio course delivered it to me in the most profound way. You may assimilate information in a different way to me.

I wanted to build my portfolio and had set myself the challenge of buying eight houses in one year. Not easy, but I had also learned 'quite possible' as long as I believed I could do it.

My two main hurdles were:

1. More customers meant more workload, which I didn't want. I could always employ someone, but no one would look after my places like I could. I didn't want to be a boss and, most importantly, I would have to get a job to afford to pay them! I needed to streamline my business, free up some more time and develop some systems to do this.

2. I was now using the income from my current portfolio to live on, so didn't have any money to put into buying new places. My usual, much loved, buy-to-let lender had announced that now I was 'self employed', I no longer met their lending criteria, thus putting an end to my current way of financing deals. Wonderful!

With my brain working better than it had for years, I punched in the questions. It gave me two answers, neither of which I expected but went along with anyway.

The first was a recipe for time. It developed slowly, but worked very well then and is still the backbone of how I leverage my time against my business. It has changed very little over the years. The way to think of this system is that you are the cordial and this system is the water. Both essential to a refreshing drink but one takes up a lot less room in the glass!

The recipe looks like this:

*   1 x giving attitude
*   1 x master key system
*   1 x answering service and multiple access points to my

company
- 2 x odd job and general maintenance person
- 2 x mobile phones
- 2 x property lawyers
- 2 x independent mortgage advisors

Giving attitude

It's important that the people in my houses feel valued and that's why it's essential to make them comfortable whilst they are there. Retention is much easier than attraction and I never know why so many landlords ignore this. Every Easter, each one of my customers receives an Easter egg or gift or some kind. They will also receive something at Christmas from me. The reason for this isn't to make friends, but to show my customers that I value their business. Also, if I haven't seen them for several months, to let them know I'm still here. Doing this takes up hardly any of my time and costs hardly anything. In fact, I regularly contact them to tell them about the great benefits they receive by living in one of my houses. For example, whilst renting from me they can:

- Book a cab with one of several local companies and receive 25% off the meter price.
- Get discounts on tyres, exhausts and servicing for their cars.
- Get discounts in coffee shops, bars and restaurants locally.
- Free gym passes.
- Get great discounts on cycles to beauty treatments

There are many more benefits that are too extensive to list but of the 150+ businesses locally that my customers can use and receive a genuine benefit over someone who doesn't rent from me, it takes no work for me to source these suppliers and doesn't cost me a penny! By starting a self perpetuating ball rolling a few years ago my customers are saving cold hard cash on their day to day living with no intervention, time or financial from me!

There are a few benefits I do offer my customers that come at a small time and financial cost to me, but for 15 minutes a month input from me and with a budget of less than £15 per person per year (which is factored into their rent so in reality is free) I can offer things like free cinema tickets for the local multiplex, breakfast or lunch on me at a local café and if they've got a sweet tooth, someone will even deliver a box of luxury cup cakes to their door!

Master key system

I have nearly two hundred locks in all of my houses, including each sharer having a lock on his or her door. Each lock has at least two spare keys.

As my portfolio grew, I would turn up at places without the right keys or, even worse, lose keys. I had a giant key ring that held all of the front door keys to my properties one end and at the other would be keys for the bedrooms, garages or whatever else I would need a key for that day. Somehow I could tell by looking at a front door key, which house it was for. This was mainly down to remembering the combination of manufacturer, key colour and shape. With the individual rooms I didn't stand a chance. I had put off buying a master key system due to the cost and hassle of changing the locks over but, after a bit of initial pain with my first supplier, the cost and effort was far outweighed by subsequent ease of life and professionalism that not carrying around a bunch of keys gives you. I now carry three keys that will operate every single front and bedroom door I have. Whether you have one house or one hundred, I can't recommend a master key system enough to you. It doesn't have to be the most secure on the market either. A basic 'off the shelf' system will work very well.

Answering service and multiple access

Contact with my business is available to my customers, potential customers and anyone else who wants to speak to me, all the time. I may only work a few hours a day and have no direct employees, but my business never closes and no one has ever guessed that I am just one guy, essentially running a very simple business system. People can email, text and call twenty-four hours a day, seven days a week and someone will get back to them. If they wish to speak to a person, they can call any time of the day or night for a chat! If they want to stop halfway through their Christmas dinner, on a bank holiday or at 3am in the morning and call us, then a real person will answer the phone.

I encourage renters to use this method to contact my company, as I prefer to look after people when they are moving in and moving out and let my 'virtual' office handle the day-to-day running of my houses along with the systems (yes, there I go again about systems) I have in place to keep them happy.

The answering service costs a couple of pounds a day, but means that any calls I don't answer are picked up by them twenty-four hours a day, seven days a week. The company who operate this for me are very professional and can handle most situations. This is yet another great time saver and has three other main benefits.

Quite often, people calling up for accommodation won't leave messages and just move on to the next advert. Even when my mobile is switched off (it diverts), they still get to speak to someone who collects all the details I have asked them to and then texts and emails it over to me.

For my existing sharers, they can call for any problem and speak to someone. They might be locked out, have a flooded kitchen, broken boiler, or faulty appliance. They only have one number to call to get any of these issues resolved. All non-urgent queries will be recorded then emailed and sent by text to me, and my answering service will deal with any emergencies. They have a list of my approved suppliers and will call them to act quickly if needed.

As I have already mentioned, I can switch my phone and PC on in the morning only to find that overnight: A kitchen had flooded, two people had locked themselves out and a boiler had packed up. All slightly perplexing, but all of these queries had been dealt with, in most cases, while I was sleeping like a baby.

Finally, because there is a very slight barrier in getting hold of me, people will more often than not try to solve a problem themselves. I would estimate that this stops about 90% of the calls that most landlords get about trivial issues. It empowers people to use their own initiative, but still gives them the security of knowing that I'm there, even if they can't speak to me straight away.

Odd job and general maintenance people

These speak for themselves and I would suggest you have one or two of each. My odd job guy does the DIY type work that would be expensive if I paid my highly skilled maintenance engineer to do, and my maintenance engineer does the jobs you need to be qualified for. I also use the latter to act as co-ordinator for all of my plumbing, carpentry and electrical jobs. This means that I only have one person to call to get any trade booked.

Two mobile phones

Yes, it's bulky and slightly inconvenient, but a lot less inconvenient than getting calls at all hours! When I'm asleep, on holiday, out for a meal or just want some peace and quiet, I simply switch my work phone off.

My answering service deals with any emergencies and I can look after the rest when I'm next in. They also have my wife's personal numbers and mine so, if they get stuck, all bases should be covered. There will be the crossover of friends that you also do business with, but make sure they know which number is which.

They will all call you at some point and say, "I know I'm

supposed to use the other number but..."

Just stop them and confirm back to them politely what THEY have just said.

My personal mobile number is a heavily guarded secret, so much so, that if it ever becomes 'too available' I'll change it.

This is a simple rule, but imperative to maintain your quality of life.

With all of the above in place, I was ready to tackle my second problem of lack of investment capital.

Throughout all of my training for my eight round epic house-buying bout, I was coming to a peak. Like a boxer before a fight, I was timing this peak to coincide with the first bell.

This was going to be in January, which was the following month.

It was me versus everyone in the city selling a house within fifteen minutes distance of mine. It was well and truly a sellers' market and, naively, I fancied my chances.

I was primed, twitchy and ready. I still didn't know how I was going to finance these houses, but it didn't matter. I just knew that I would succeed.

I was almost right.

CHAPTER ELEVEN

FLOAT LIKE A BUTTERFLY...

There were now several lenders in the market who would let you get round some of the 10-15% deposit they wanted you to put down. This was generally done in either of two ways:

A Vendor Paid Deposit

This is normally where the person/company you are buying from will pay some of your deposit for you. A working example would be:

You find a property that will value (for easy maths) at £100,000. However, the vendor agrees to accept £95,000 for it.

You buy the property for £100,000 with a 15% deposit but, in real terms, only put down 10%, as the other five is made up by the vendor 'gifting' you an imaginary £5,000. The lender is happy as the valuer they've employed has confirmed the 'open market value' is £100,000. The vendor is happy as they have sold their property, and you are happy as you have saved yourself a few thousand pounds.

A Vendor Paid Cash Back

This works in very much the same way as a vendor paid deposit but, instead of the vendor paying some of the deposit, you pay it all and the vendor gives you back a percentage of the property's value on completion. This is arranged with the lender's knowledge so there are no breaches of the mortgage terms and the solicitors arrange the cash back, meaning that there is no chance of the vendor running off with your money.

I found that many lenders would accept one of these techniques, but never both, and would only go up to 5% in total, meaning that I had still to put 10% in.

Although helpful to some, this didn't really help me!

January started well and I found plenty of houses to buy, but couldn't raise a deposit.

February started just as well and I found even more houses, but still couldn't raise a deposit.

March and April were seeing the property market really starting to pick up, and I was having trouble fitting all the viewings in. I was still finding plenty of houses I liked but still hitting the same brick wall. I was beginning to lose hope.

I was still pushing hard and looking for financing options but every door was closed. Then, in a moment of near exasperation, and with all doors firmly shut, I stumbled across an open window!

During all of my property research and time spent being a landlord, a particular investment company kept cropping up over and over again.

Their advertisements basically told people that absolutely anyone could be a property millionaire, that there was no skill required and for just a few thousand pounds, they would teach you everything you needed to know in a weekend.

Then, if you were too busy to look for properties, they had loads of fantastic 'off plan' deals to choose from, home and abroad. They would help with all the financing so you didn't need to understand that either and could just sit back, put your feet up and rake it in. After all, it's just like Monopoly, right?

People were flocking to this company and there were now thousands of 'Armchair Investors' boasting to their friends at dinner parties about the lovely little duplex they had just bought in Florida. Before and after the company eventually folded, many of these investors had lost everything from their 'play money' to life savings, pensions and even family homes.

Many found that rental forecasts were greatly inflated and they were left 'topping up' each cash cow by a few hundred pounds a month. A lot of the 'off plan' properties were so far ahead of even being started, let alone completed and only factored in double digit price rises for the future. Many innocent people lost large deposits as well as facing legal action when they couldn't borrow what they needed against their investment when it was finally finished.

Although I was desperate to find out if there were any gems of information or deals this company could offer me, I had two main reasons for not handing them any money. I didn't understand why it cost so much to learn all this information and, as I already had several properties, wondered if I could figure out a way forward for free on my own.

Also, this idea seemed to be to property investment what diet milk-shakes are to losing weight. Yes, if you drink the shakes you will lose weight, but it won't teach you anything about good nutrition or address the real reason for being overweight in the first place. Can losing weight this way ultimately be successful for life? For most, I don't think so. And I don't think that becoming a property investor on a diet of daytime television shows and a weekend with this company could work either.

In most cases, learning more about less will make you richer. An example of this is your GP. He or she should have a very good overall knowledge of the human body and how it works, etc. However, if your GP had then gone on to specialise in one area, such as the brain; then he or she would have learned more information about less of the body and, if they had done it right, increased their lucrative power.

I once made the mistake of thinking that because I was a good property investor and landlord, I would automatically be a good property developer as well.

I proceeded to buy a tired studio apartment and turn it into a one bedroom flat. I put in an extra window in the bed-sitter part and put a stud wall up, dividing the room in two, thus giving the place a separate bedroom and living area.

My builder did the job for me and, through my poor calculations, finished 20% over budget. The place was so small that if you had put your front door key in too quickly you might have broken the back window, but it looked immaculate.

The three estate agents I got in to value the place praised me on the quality of finish and enthused about how nice it looked, but they all dropped the same bombshell. I had added less to the value of the flat than I had just paid for having the work done!

The reasons were that there had been no need to spend so much at the bottom of the market. I had paid too much for it to start with and there's only so much you can do with a small space.

I rented it out for a year and then sold it on the back of the rises in market and made a tidy profit. It rented well but I wanted the money for another place.

Anyway, back to my open window.

For some reason, which I still don't comprehend, this company had made a video of one of their courses. An unscrupulous scoundrel then put it onto half a dozen DVD's and was selling it for the price of a pizza on Ebay. Result!

The version I had was in real time so I sat in my lounge for two days, drinking coffee and eating biscuits, watching a load of wide-eyed novices listening to some blokes, who looked like ex double glazing or door-to-door salesmen, telling them that there's nothing as secure as property, which would always double in value every seven years, and that there was such a shortage of land in this country that even if there were an economic downturn, property prices would, at worst, level off.

I felt very sorry for these people as most didn't own any property and, by the words they were using, it was obvious that many had borrowed the money to be on the course.

As I didn't want to miss anything, I watched the whole thing, wired on coffee and covered in hobnob crumbs.

About halfway through the second day, I was eating my lunch while at the same time watching a large Nigerian man cramming sausage rolls and mini pizzas into his mouth, when he turned to the person next to him and, barely audible over the booming voice of the trainer, half said and half sprayed:

"Did you know that xxxx has just started accepting vendor paid deposit as well as vendor paid cashback on the same deal? They're also offering eighty-nine percent loan to value mortgages."

I could see that this information, along with some mini pizza, had gone straight over the head of the person next to him, but this was just what I needed!

I watched the rest of the DVD, which was painful, and then called my mortgage advisor. Initially adamant that no lender in their right mind would agree to something like that, he eventually phoned them and confirmed that this was true.

Before he could put the phone down, I was surfing the net, trawling the local rag and chatting up every estate agent I could get on the phone or in front of me.

It was now May and I was still in the changing room waiting to be called up to the ring. Importantly, I hadn't given up or stopped training and could take on almost any fight at short notice.
"Ding, ding!"

Round One

I found a property that, even in a fast moving market, had been up for sale for nearly a year with no takers. The owner had emigrated years ago and was just selling off his UK properties. He was out of touch with its true value; the agent had also undervalued it and not bothered to update the price as the months went on. It had an interesting person who was a bit of a hoarder and had only five teeth.

I called the agent who I knew reasonably well from putting myself about, and he told me that the reason it hadn't been snapped up was because the person living there was paying a very low rent and was on an old style 'Assured Tenancy' and not what most landlords would use today, which would be an 'Assured Short

Hold Tenancy'

I didn't know much about this type of tenancy and it seemed that most other landlords didn't either. The main perception was that it was practically impossible to get rid of someone who had an 'Assured Tenancy' and even putting their rent up was difficult. They could also force landlords to carry out works on the property in complete peace of mind that if they upset their landlord, they couldn't be asked to leave.

As it was so hard to get the person out of the house once they were in, most lenders wouldn't lend against the property, as they too would be stuck with the occupant if they ever had to repossess it.

From my bank days, I even remember a lady who I helped invest over twenty thousand pounds that a landlord had paid to buy her out of the assured tenancy that her deceased parents had taken out years before!

In short, if you are a landlord: Assured Short Hold Tenancies (or AST) – Fair(ish) to all parties. Assured Tenancies (or AT) – Run away!

Being curious, I had a look anyway.

The place was a bit shabby, but the lady living there was very pleasant and we got on well. She even gave me a copy of her tenancy agreement to take away, which was nice.

I had a look over it in the car and to me, it just looked like a normal AST. Because of this I forwarded it to my property lawyer to see if she could explain the differences so that I didn't get caught out with one of these in the future.

She called me the next day to say there weren't any differences in this case, as it wasn't an AT but a normal AST. I asked her to double-check it, which she did and reconfirmed that it was a standard tenancy. I trust her implicitly, but still got a second opinion.

It was confirmed to be an AST and with this great news I decided to keep my mouth shut and buy the place!

With the help of my new favourite lenders' 'flexible' deposit terms I managed to negotiate a 5% vendor paid deposit plus 5% cashback on completion, meaning that I only had to put in 1% of the purchase price plus legal cost.

I had a long chat with the lady living there who was happy not to have the place in showroom condition and in return would pay a reduced rent for it. With all parties happy, the deal came together very well.

There was some confusion on the deeds, however, which I didn't mention until after completion. The plot of land on the document was outlined in red but there was also a little red box outlined around the corner from the house.

My property lawyer had already told me that this was a garage, but it had not been mentioned by the sellers' side and, when I went to pick the keys up from the estate agent, he told me there definitely wasn't one.

After a little game of 'garage pantomime' with my side saying, "Oh, yes there is" and the other side saying, "Oh, no there isn't" The agent finally managed to get hold of the vendor who confirmed that in fact there was a garage, but he didn't know where the keys were so hadn't bothered mentioning it!

All in all, a fantastic first round.

Round Two

This was a new-build four-bedroom property that I had seen advertised by another 'diet shake' buying club. Basically, they would go around offering to bulk sell properties, at a large discount, for builders who were unable to sell themselves. They would then pass the houses on to property novices, telling them that they would rent out easily, and charge them a few thousand pounds to broker the deal.

The main problems here, and what these companies never mention, is that they are only offering these properties for sale as the builders, who are themselves experts at selling houses, weren't able to sell them.

As these places were ten minutes from my house, I visited the sales office to have a look around a few of the ten properties they had given to the buying club, to find out why they weren't selling. They were in an affluent part of the city and overlooked a picturesque lake.

There was a modern shopping centre within a two-minute walk and future plans to build bars, restaurants and shops close enough to be an asset but not a nuisance, although this information wasn't widely known.

The site was ideal but the main problems were due to a planning error of some kind, which I never did quite get to the bottom of. Even though the houses were constructed correctly, they were forced to sell them as three-beds with a study and not four-beds; although some of the studies were the size of large double bedrooms! This meant that when people were looking for properties, they were being asked to pay four-bedroom prices for what they thought were three-bed houses. As a result many didn't even bother looking round. The houses also had a medium-sized lounge diner which would be considered small for a family home and, finally, the kitchens were slightly smaller than most others in the neighbourhood. The other hurdle was that, although on paper the rent would cover the mortgage, anyone who did the tiniest bit of research would find that there was a massive oversupply of houses of this type in the area, so in reality, a landlord could expect about 10-15% less than market value for the rent.

My unique buying point was that I was planning to rent this house out as an executive house share, meaning that even on conservative calculations it would be cash positive by a few hundred pounds each month.

I tried to sweet talk the builder into giving me the same discount they were offering through the broker but, as an individual, they sent me packing.

Knowing I could structure the deal in a similar way to the last property, as the discounts were very good and I was happy with the reasons why others weren't snapping them up, I reluctantly paid the broker their finders' fee and bought one.

The broker had sold all ten of these houses but, as the deals progressed, it was obvious that the relationship between the broker, the builder and some of the clients was unravelling. As I was local, I stopped talking to the broker completely and started to speak directly to the builder, which we both preferred. There was a four-week deadline for completion and I could see that it wouldn't happen unless I worked directly with the organ grinder and not his adopted monkey. It also helped me build a very good relationship with them.

My house completed four weeks and three days after it all started and I was apologetic that I'd missed the four-week deadline.

They were fine about it, especially as they could see how much work I had put into getting it all through and, even though I was very slightly late, I was the first person they gave the keys to.

I advertised the property as an executive house share and got everything delivered to furnish the whole house from Argos. From forks to fridge freezers, they sell them all, and at a good price. You can furnish a whole house in one or two deliveries from them, which I was now doing for all of my places.

The rooms rented out well and the cash flow, although around half of what it was from my more working class areas, was still good. The work in managing them was less, as the sharers were mainly graduates and new build houses have various guarantees; so in the unlikely event of things going wrong, I didn't have to fix it.

I was still feeling fresh and felt like I could go fifty rounds if I had to.

Round Three
Over the last few years setting up my core business of house

shares, I had built well over fifty beds, wardrobes, bedside cabinets, and chests of drawers and put up more curtains than I care to remember (bearing in mind that each house had up to ten windows).

I was now getting an odd-job guy in to do the work and paying by the task, not the day, to keep his speed up.

I kept in touch with the house builders' sales office, even though mine had completed, as they were getting more and more fed up with the buying club. I'd had my house for nearly four weeks and no one else had managed to complete his or her purchase.

To cover this, the buying club was trying to put this back onto the builder, by saying that all the houses were to have washer-dryers and not just washing machines, but the builder wasn't having any of it.

I empathized with the sales team, telling them that it was a trivial matter and the club should just get over it, and dropped off some flowers and chocolates as a thank you to them. As I was paying the utilities on these houses, not having a dryer was better for me anyway; I didn't want an expensive dryer running for an hour just to dry a pair of someone's 'lucky pants' on a Saturday night!

The next day I got a call from the area sales manager saying that they were pulling out of one of the sales as the buyer and club had missed their fifth deadline to complete. They would offer me exactly the same deal as on my existing one and I wouldn't have to pay another finders' fee to that crappy buying club. Result!

I used the same lender as for the last house and they were happy for me to use the same searches, as the property was only a couple of doors away from mine. My mortgage broker, property lawyer and I sprung into action and two weeks later picked up the keys!

All my training was falling into place and I was feeling unstoppable!

Round Four

Like a kid on the way back from Alton Towers, I was happy but starting to tire; the deals were coming very close together now so it was hard to balance my finances, fill the new place and manage my existing portfolio.

I wouldn't (and still won't) let someone move into one of my houses without vetting them myself, so was spending a lot of time on viewings.

I then got a call from Matilda, an estate agent I had been working with. She had a house on her books for which the buyer wanted a quick sale, but was proving difficult to shift.

I 'Columbo'd' the area and got to the bottom of why.

The house was originally a three-bed in a working class area, but had been extended to a large luxury four-bed. The en-suite was bigger than most family bathrooms and even had a jacuzzi!

The reason why the house wasn't selling was that, not only was it one of a kind in the area, but the surrounding houses and local population were much more modest. I imagine that even when it was a three-bed, it would have been one of the best houses in the street and, as any property investor will advise, you should ALWAYS buy the worst house in the best street and not the other way round.

I decided that this rule was a 'mostly' and not an 'always' and put an offer in.

Even though it was a four-bed, it had a separate dining room so I could rent the lounge out as bedroom five, turn the dining room into the lounge, use the conservatory as a dining room, as well as putting some stools under the breakfast bar in the large kitchen.

The owner had split with her husband and the proceeds of the sale would end the last tie they had. It was clear that the upkeep was a lot for her, and her new partner had little interest in looking after a house when half of any proceeds were going to her ex. She was also eight months pregnant.

I found out that I could borrow 85% of its mortgage valuation and, although not happy, the vendor accepted my offer. She was in danger of losing another house and I got the impression she just wanted rid of the place, along with its associated memories.

I used the same technique as I'd used in rounds one and two and the sale proceeded at a good pace.

The house filled up at a reasonable rate and some very good people moved in. To this day it's my best house for time versus profit. It only needed a bit of a tidy up and the only real problem was a cat that would run into the house whenever anyone opened a door or window. Initially the vendor said it wasn't hers, but eventually owned up and came to collect it.

I had used up a lot of energy in the first four rounds and was starting to puff and blow a bit.

Round Five

Round five overlapped rounds three and four, so I was performing a *Cirque de Soleil* style juggling act with my purchases; physically I was tired and mentally, I was getting confused.

The house builders' area sales manager had called again to say that they had pulled out of a sale with another one of the buying club's investors, so I wiped the sweat off, picked up another ball and smiled at the audience.

Round Six

Round six was a flurry of punches and, battered and bruised, I was now fighting on instinct. I wasn't enjoying this any more and was under the most pressure I had ever experienced in my life. I somehow found myself in a two-bed starter home that an agent had put me onto and I'd said I would buy. It was in a small cul-de-sac of identical properties and the area had a good feel about it. Once again, I was lucky enough to have a motivated seller and had structured the deal for a very low amount of cash in, so just said, "I'll have it".

When I picked up the keys from the agent, my mind was spinning so much I couldn't even remember where the house was. To top it off, when I got there I discovered that there was no central heating and that the wooden window frames had seen much better days. The rent barely covered the mortgage and it was obvious I hadn't researched it properly.

The exit from the cul-de-sac was also straight onto a busy dual carriageway and the bus stop was a twenty minute walk away, with the local shops on the other side of the road.

I had let my guard down, been caught flush with an uppercut and was now taking a count.

When I got up, I held on for dear life and was able to recover the situation slightly. I offered the house to a selection of my best sharers. These were people who paid their rent well, had been with me for at least six months, were clean and tidy, but who I suspected would never pass a credit check from a letting agent, or have the fees associated with the large deposits being asked for.

They would happily pay above market rent because of this. The deposit was a month's rent of which I was already holding around half from the room they currently rented and would let them make up the rest over a couple of months.

A surprising amount of people jumped at the offer, so I chose the best applicant.

Eighteen months later, the bus route changed slightly to incorporate the area and the council lowered the road's speed limit and put a pelican crossing over the dual carriageway. This was a sheer fluke and in no way pre -empted by me at any point.

I'd lost this round, well and truly but had managed to close the margin but was barely still in the fight.

Round Seven

By the start of August, I was seeing stars and embarking on my seventh purchase in four months. Buying one house was hard enough, but having three or four on the go at once wasn't simply three or four times more difficult, I was finding it about ten times harder.

A call came in from the house builder again to say that all but one of the houses had gone through, so would I like the one that was left.

I wanted to say no, but they were renting out well and the price was very good, so I went for it.

Luckily, my team were able to get this one through with minimal input from me as I was dead on my feet. Metaphorically, my legs were gone and I hadn't fully recovered from the last round.

I somehow lasted to the bell.

My new executive house shares were renting out to scientists, doctors, teachers and many other professionals, but the 'single let' landlords weren't so lucky.

Within a year of buying, and with rents not covering mortgages and, in some cases, with only 50% occupancy, four of the six houses that I hadn't bought were up for sale and, even in a rising market, were being offered at 90-95% of their original gross price. This was still higher than the net price we had all paid but I think those that did sell would have lost most of their gains, if not all, on lost rent.

No one had told the buyers that, like new cars, new houses carry a premium too. You may not lose the same money as when you drive your shiny new motor off the forecourt, but people who want a new house, will buy a new house for top money and not a slightly used one.

Round Eight

It was the start of September and I still had three months left to buy my final house. Plenty of time you would have thought, right!

The bell rang but there was nothing left in me. I had given up and quit on my stool. I had nothing more to give. I had been drained mentally and physically like never before. What started as fun and exciting had turned into a chore, then a tyrant then, worse still, a job!

I looked at the other goals I had set myself for the year and had achieved. Like my property purchases, I had written them down on paper without the means or knowledge to get them done, but I had.

My income was now double what I'd been earning at the bank and I was working a third of the time but the intensity was too much to handle. I was surly, irritable and not much fun to be around.

I picked up my own towel, threw it in the centre of the ring and went off for a very long shower.

For at least the rest of the year I didn't want to hear about houses for sale, so I told all of my contacts that I wasn't buying and went back to running my business, getting the service back on track and finished renting out the two houses, twenty-one new rooms and five garages that came with them (I never miss a chance to rent something out!).

Eventually, the dust settled along with my stress levels and working past 1.pm became a late day for me again.

I remembered once again why I'd signed up for this!

CHAPTER 12

PHEW!

I had planned to take just three months off from buying houses; instead I had gotten comfortable and lazy. It was over nine months on and I was still twiddling my thumbs.

In corporate terms, my work/life balance was just about right and, if I'm completely honest, the intensity of buying seven houses in five months had taken more of a toll than I had first thought. Although my drive had returned, I wasn't particularly active in looking for new places and my profile had dropped considerably around the contacts whose lists my name topped whenever a good deal came along.

As I was out of the spotlight, I was also out of practice and, when balls were thrown my way, I was fumbling them or taking too long to analyse deals and thereby losing out. There were also now plenty of people willing to put more money in than I was, as well as accepting less return.

Around the middle of the year, one of my old contacts was feeling sorry for me and gave me a good head start on a cheap one-bedroom flat.

I'd always avoided one-bedroom flats, as a mate of mine who was also a landlord as well as a letting agent and, at the same time, one of my mentors, had advised me to avoid them.

According to him, one-bedroom flats were generally stepping-stones for people and they would always be looking for something better. This would mean that my turnover would be higher along with wear, tear and voids. He generally stuck to three bedroom places, which he told me let well across the board. He seemed to know what he was talking about so, without any investigation on my part, his view became my view. I had listened to him and up until then, like a complete idiot, had always dismissed one-bedroom flats.

Property investing, along with most other things in life, is about 'horses for courses'. He'd been talking to me about 'his ideals' and 'his investment' strategy and I had listened blindly.

In turn, I had completely overlooked a massive opportunity for my business. For years, a large percentage of my sharers would regularly come to me for places when they were looking to 'trade up'. Quite often my two and three-bed places were either too big or out of their price range. They were ideally looking for a one-bedroom place, which I was avoiding, as there was no market for them!

A flippant piece of advice and my own stupidity had prevented me from maximizing a massive opportunity for my own business over the last five years or so, and I could have kicked myself.

With the excitement of this revelation, along with the fact that the flat was cheap, I bought it. The place had been empty for the last two years but, unlike a house, had not deteriorated too badly. It was on the middle floor of a three-storey block of twelve so wasn't really exposed to the elements and normal decay that a house would have been.

The owner had been living with his girlfriend for the last two years and had kept it 'just in case'. They were now engaged with a baby on the way and selling the flat would pay for a wedding and a people carrier.

The local area had new-build flats springing up everywhere and the developers were throwing in all sorts of incentives to first time buyers and investors, so a fifteen-year-old smelly flat in need of some tender loving care wasn't lighting any fires. To make it even more ugly, nearly all the second-hand flats were in tip-top condition and those that weren't were being bought by developers cheaply, magnolia'd up to the eyeballs and then turned around in an afternoon.

This flat was too ugly for most first time buyers and not cheap enough for most investors to make a large enough return; so although still somewhat out of shape, I waddled in and bought it.

I chose a mortgage company that would let me remortgage three months after completion to get most of my money back out; I got a good discount from the vendor and picked up the keys a few weeks later.

Once again I offered it to my best customers and, to my amazement, none of them wanted it. I had forgotten to advertise the flat to them 'during' the buying process to create a buzz and some healthy competition. Subsequently, my enthusiasm was met with indifference.

A couple of days after I had picked up the keys, I got a call from the local council, asking me if I could help someone who was about to become homeless.

I immediately said, "Nope!"

I had half a dozen renters who had ended up on housing benefit, but had a strict rule never to take anyone who was on benefits at the time they wanted to move in. My customers who had found themselves on hard times and had the DSS paying their rent, included a milkman who had somehow fallen out of his float and broken his pelvis, an office worker who had been laid off and then got addicted to daytime telly and also a checkout girl from one of the more budget supermarkets. She had not only developed repetitive strain injury from continually scanning cans of 'Tennents', (there is an overlooked irony that this is the lager of choice for so many homeless people) but the 'beeping' from the barcode reader had also given her some kind of post traumatic stress disorder.

There was also the added hassle that the council sometimes took several months to agree a housing benefit claim and then paid it in arrears, meaning landlords had to pay the mortgage and then wait for reimbursement. To make matters worse, if the claimant even sneezed, they would suspend their claim while they looked into whether this denoted a 'change of circumstances' which meant a landlord would then have to wait several more weeks to get paid.

I'd had two previous circumstances where the day before a claimant's rent was due to be paid, which was already four weeks after its due date, I got a letter saying that they weren't getting any money, meaning I was already one month behind and would have to wait another two months before they could be legally evicted!

The government had also decided that they wouldn't pay the rent directly to the landlords but to the claimants, which often meant that someone already slightly vulnerable, might suddenly get what equated to several weeks' benefit money dumped into their account and it was now up to them to take this money from their bank and walk past a few bookies, pubs, clothes shops and other distractions before putting the money into my bank.

Today though, I had an empty flat and the person on the other end of the phone was actually a very good salesperson. Along with my frustration of how the rents were paid, my experience of council office workers was that they were mainly made up of union protected suits who would themselves go on the sick at the drop of a hat (on full pay of course) and, if they were off work for more than half a day, would demand a three week retraining course. Otherwise, they always seemed to be on some health and safety programme about 'sitting on a chair correctly' or 'the dangers of not picking up an empty box properly'. I always wondered how much more efficient council offices would run if they had shareholders to answer to and not tax payers.

I'm glad to say that my narrow views have since widened somewhat and I now work with some very nice folk at the council.

The person they were looking for me to house, had run several moderately successful businesses, but a freak car accident meant that he was now unable to work and his old accommodation had lapsed whilst he was in hospital.

Call me a sucker but I agreed to meet the guy.

Rex was early for our meeting, which was a very good start, and had a suit on which also helped. It was at least three sizes too big for him, and made him look like a 1970's police detective, but I was glad he had made an effort. When I asked him about the suit, he told me he had borrowed it from another church member and apologised for the style and that it was so ill-fitting.

Being early, wearing a suit and, although I don't attend any church, the fact that he did gave me somewhat of an insight into his values. His injuries meant that he walked slowly and struggled with the stairs to the first floor flat, and I admired his determination and pride.

His insides were pretty messed up from the accident and the housing officer had mentioned that even a mild fall could kill him. I liked Rex but wasn't sure I could do with the stress of this, but I was here now. I moved all obstacles as we walked round, made sure the doors didn't slam and prayed he stayed upright.

He loved the place and tried to give me a deposit there and then, but I wanted to check his references out. I normally go on gut feeling with people and, although I liked him, was doing all I could not to give him a place. His references didn't help with this, as one was from his vicar, the next was from a high-ranking police officer and the last was from someone who had just got a MBE for their services to the community.

I googled them all, did all I could to check their legitimacy and they all spoke very highly of Rex, so I gave in and let him have the place.

His housing benefit covered 90% of the rent and I agreed to waive the rest if he took it as it was. I did this, as even if he stayed for two years, it would still be cheaper for me than if I had tarted the place up, along with the fact that if he was a 'wrong un' I wouldn't be too upset if he broke things that were due for replacement anyway.

I dropped by unannounced about two months later and my jaw almost hit the floor when I saw the condition of the place. Not only was the flat spotlessly clean, Rex had recarpeted most of it and painted the walls in a very nice colour. He had deep cleaned the kitchen and bathroom which now looked almost new and, I would say, added about 5% to the flat's value.

I was sad when Rex left a few months later to fulfil his dream of living on a narrow boat. I was even sadder when he called a week later to say that he had made a huge mistake by moving out, and I had to tell him that someone else was already benefiting from the work he had put in on the flat.

I stayed in touch with him for a while but nothing came up that was suitable for him and we eventually lost touch. I learned that he had lent his phone to someone in need so they could receive calls about jobs they were applying for, but they had disappeared with it along with some money he had also lent them. About three years later, Rex managed to get back in touch with me and is still with me today.

The next house was an easy one. We were living in a large four-bedroom townhouse that was a tiny plot. The garden, which was the biggest on the estate, was about half the size of the land that the house stood on. With a baby on the way, we decided that a place with a garden and not a postage stamp was essential, so we moved and rented the place out.

It rents out very well as an executive house share, has a cash flow of several hundred pounds a month and is very close to an area about to have several million pounds of riverside leisure facilities built. It meant we had a larger mortgage on our next home, but the cash flow from the old one more than makes up for it.

After the stresses of the last year, I had set myself the very lazy target of buying only two houses during the following twelve months.

It was July; I had done this, so I put my feet up. A new house that needed work, adjustments to being a father and a couple of problem housemate were enough to keep me busy for now.

I saw that my favourite national house builder was building again and lazily asked them for the same 15% discounts that I'd had before, which they flatly declined as in their words:

"We can't build 'em quick enough".

I was slightly perplexed, but not enough to lose any sleep over it.

By December, however, the tables had turned somewhat.

I sometimes get several calls per week from other landlords who've thought running house shares to be easy money, bought them too far away from where they live, or just got tired of running them and are looking for someone else to do it.

I always politely decline as, not only do I not want to commit time to grow someone else's business, but in the past have had more trouble from those landlords than the people in their houses and don't want to associate my company name with it. Never one to miss out on an opportunity though, I struck up an agreement with a good local letting agent and we have a 80/20 split on all commissions and charges they get from landlords I pass their way, so I get paid each and every month a growing amount of money by simply saying, "Im sorry I can't help, but I'll get someone to call you who can."

Yes, it's that easy and the landlord, the letting agent and I are all very happy with the agreement.

I had, however, started meeting with a couple of landlords for a pint on a monthly basis and, after a while, our group had grown to twenty or thirty people. We decided to call ourselves the 'Peterborough Property Investors Group' which somehow got shortened to PetPIG.org when the website was launched.

Meeting other landlords is a great way to share stories, information, good tradesmen, etc, and keep abreast of what's going on locally; I strongly recommend you do the same in your area.

My only caveat was that for every piece of advice I gave someone, I would expect something back of equal value and vice-versa, of course. When it became obvious that people just wanted to copy what I was doing without offering anything in return, I would excuse myself and talk to someone else. I remember telling another landlord who was taking up most of my time at the meetings and not contributing anything:

"Look, what do you think my local chippy would do if I walked in and asked him the best way to go into direct competition with him, yet had nothing to offer him in exchange?"

It took a while for the penny to drop, and I'm now happy to work with him.

At one of the meetings, a landlord for whom I have a lot of respect flippantly told me that my favourite national house builder was now offering 15% off the houses they had given me the boot on back in July.

I was still feeling lazy and had met my very soft target of two houses for the year, so the information only half stuck.

What did stick, however, was the fact that they hadn't told me about their new offers, especially as we had worked so well together the year before.

Like a jealous spouse, I wanted to know why they were now flirting with this other landlord and not me! What did he have that I didn't? Was he better looking? Had I let myself go? Maybe I had become a bit set in my ways.

I brooded all night and then rang them in the morning, of course pretending that nothing was wrong and I was fine, really.

The situation wasn't quite as bad as I thought. The old sales team there had all left since my last purchases and, because I hadn't bothered to keep my profile up with the new team, none of them had even heard of me.

I had a shave, sucked in my belly, sprayed on some Brut and educated them on how well things had gone with the last four houses I had bought from them, which the local office confirmed, and we were back in business.

The reasons they were now offering the 15% were that although they had built some very nice four-bedroom executive houses:

1. The site didn't even have a proper road in, so even though the houses were in a very affluent and growing area of the city they were, for now, in the middle of nowhere, as the local shops, bars and local transport services weren't in place. If you imagine writing the numbers one to ten on a piece of paper; then the rest of the development had been built so far from one to three that their houses were clustered at number six. Areas four and five were just mud.

2. The houses were finished but empty, so essentially tying up cash flow, as the previous buyer had pulled out at the last minute.

3. It was their year end and the local area office was just off its target and the directors just might miss their big bonuses.

They offered me eight houses in total: four each of three-beds and four-beds. I liked them all but the three-beds didn't stack up for rentals so I declined those.

I managed to get a very good rapport going with the area sales manager, along with the people on site, and established that if I bought the large four-beds they would still get their fat cat bonuses and I could have 15% off.

I tried my luck and we settled on a 20% discount provided I could complete in four weeks; they would even throw in the kitchen appliances, carpets in two of them, along with integrated sound systems. I didn't know how I was going to structure this and, if it came off, the rooms would be ready at the end of December. A hard time to let one room let alone sixteen, but I agreed anyway.

My houses were still having the second fixes, kitchens and bathrooms put in, but I managed to let enough of the rooms to cover the running costs of the properties before getting the keys. This was down to the site having a show home. It was the same layout as the other houses but just 'glammed up' to the eyeballs. I spent weeks walking round it with blue bags on my shoes showing it off to prospective housemates.

The slightly tricky part was the financing. The techniques I had used last year were no longer available and, although I had some very healthy discounts in place, I didn't have the cash to cover one of the deposits let alone four!

It was time to:

Take it to the Bridge

A bridging loan is essentially that: a 'financial bridge' from one place to the other; it was going to span the gap in my own finances in buying these houses and, if I got it right, pay for all my legal costs, stamp duty and furnishings.

I set my trusty mortgage advisor to work looking for a lender and bridging company who would work together.

He found one that was about to stop accepting deals structured in this way by the end of the week, but would honour applications that were already in.

I jumped in the car and headed for his office, briefly stopping on the way to look at a one-bedroom ex council flat that an agent had put me on to. As with all the ex-council flats I had seen, it was at least 25% bigger than most new builds and, in this case, less than half the price. Bizarrely, this flat had a cupboard that was 9ft x 8ft which was bigger than most modern kitchens. It didn't have a window in it so I decided that, at some point, I would make this into a kitchen and turn the 20ft x 10ft kitchen diner into a second bedroom. This would not only increase the rent, as it would have two large double bedrooms, it would also add value.

Once again this was a 'seller in love' and he wanted to get shot of the place quickly so that he could spend his capital growth on his new love. He was also worried about the market crashing as the news was forecasting doom and gloom. I said I was worried too, and he agreed to knock 20% off the price.

I sat in my mortgage advisor's office for what seemed like a week. It was only about three hours, but I wasn't used to sitting still for that long any more, and being in an office always reminded me of having a job!

It was vital we got these deals right as the door was closing on the financing, so we had to make sure all the 't's were crossed and 'i's were dotted, especially as it was slightly complicated. I was applying for remortgages and not mortgages on these properties, with the lender happy to lend me 80% of the flat's market value and 85% of the houses' value. Although I didn't yet own the properties, the mortgage lender was comfortable with me buying them on a bridging loan initially, so that I then owned them and would remortgage them as soon as possible. Timing was essential on this as the bridging finance costs on each unit were the same for every twenty-four hours as each mortgage would be for a month!

The best way I can describe how this system was to work is like this: Imagine an athlete running a 100-metre race but instead of a finish line there is a very heavy door for which he hasn't got a key. He needs to run the race in record time so can't ease off towards the finish line but, at the same time, values his health and good looks. Ten metres before the door, a little fellow jumps in front of the runner with a key and opens the door letting him through. This has to be timed perfectly, as if the little fellow starts running too soon, the runner will overtake him and hit the door, and if he starts too late, he won't have time to turn the key and the runner will hit the door.

The runner is the remortgage.

The little fellow is the bridging finance.

The applications went in on the Wednesday and on Friday: SLAM! The lender pulls this type of financing on any new applicants but says they will honour mine – phew!

As you can probably guess, the road to creative financing is very rarely straight or smooth.

The Houses

The four houses moved along at a very good pace. In most cases, the house builders want you to use the mortgage advisors and legal teams they appoint, but I always use my own. They know how I work, I trust them and they are used to dealing with my unorthodox ways and short attention span.

The houses all had garages that weren't connected to the house, which meant there was a ground rent to pay. The garages also had electric gates to them and the fifty houses on this part of the site were responsible for 2% of the cost of the upkeep of these.

This wasn't particularly unusual on modern estates like this, but the house builder had slipped up a bit. The paperwork they wanted me to sign stated that I was responsible for 20% of this upkeep per house and not 2%, meaning that my four houses, which made up 8% of the development, could be liable for 80% of any future maintenance.

They had also not got the full consent of the planning office for the houses to be occupied. Several units had been sold using the builders' recommended property lawyer and this hadn't been picked up on.

My favourite national house builder's view was:

"Ah, don't worry about it. Your team are just a bit picky. These details are so small no one will ever pick up on them".

The lenders view was:

"If people can't live in them, we're not lending on them".

Luckily, the house builder sorted these problems out quickly and we were back on track.

Meanwhile, that flat was ticking along nicely but I hadn't followed it as closely as I would normally do as I'd been busy with the four houses and, after all, it was only a one-bedroom flat.

Buying five houses at once was not only hard; once again, it was very stressful. I was relieved when the day of completion came and was looking forward to taking a few days off...

Suddenly, it all unravelled.

I hadn't been paying attention; my mortgage advisor was on holiday and somehow the word 'mortgage' crept into the process instead of 'remortgage' and 'vendor paid deposit' had been used instead of 'bridging finance'. I wasn't sure how this had happened, but knew they were minor details that could be quickly dealt with. But they weren't. A little snowball had been created and was growing in speed and size at a ridiculous rate.

Rather than accept that a mistake had been made on our side, the lender pulled the mortgage offers the day before completion.

My, up until now, super slick machine ground to an embarrassing halt and we sat arguing on the hard shoulder over who had forgotten to check the oil.

A senior underwriter then got involved, accepted that we had made a simple wording error, but said that even with the correct wording they didn't lend in that manner any more anyway.

He refused to accept that the application had been in on time and flatly declined to lend.

My legal team, mortgage advisor (who'd had the last day of his holiday ruined by me phoning him fifteen times), and even the lender's own sales manager teamed up to put a huge amount of pressure on the underwriter and left him no choice but to agree to give us one of three answers:

1. Yes, you can have the money but we don't want to give it to you.
2. No, you can't have the money. On your bike, son.
3. No, you can't have the money. On your bike son, and if we are in breach of our own 'be fair to your customers' policy then you can get the financial rozzers onto us.

That afternoon, the lender's parent company issued a liquidation warning and they chose option 3.

We had fought valiantly but it was time to admit defeat. My mortgage advisor told me that he would give them a Paddington

Bear 'hard stare' in the form of a strongly-worded letter and I told the house builder we were beat.

I had just emailed the estate agent to tell them the flat was off too, and was dialling my solicitor to give her the bad news when my mobile rang. I could see it was my mortgage advisor; I was too hacked off with the situation to speak to him, but when I answered the phone was speechless to hear the good news!

Another senior underwriter had picked up my mortgage advisor's letter and called him to find out what all the fuss was. As far as she was concerned everything was fine and the money could be sent over first thing in the morning if we still wanted it. Result!

On the day of completion, I purchased the houses on the bridging loan just after 9.am and the remortgage paid off the bridge by lunchtime.

As I had bought the houses for 80% of their market valuation and the remortgage took hold at 85% in less than three hours, I got four lots of 5% back on each one which more than covered all the associated costs. By the time the dust had settled, I had completed on five houses in less than five minutes and life was good!

One of my sharers moved into the flat the next day and I filled the remainder of the sixteen rooms over the next few weeks.

EPILOGUE

FRANK BRUNO, PYGMY GOATS AND THE SERENE BEAUTY OF THE MCDONALD'S DRIVE THROUGH.

I use the techniques in this book every day to help make my sharers' occupancy as comfortable and pleasurable as possible. However, most of the strategies I formerly used to buy my houses are currently unavailable.

Now, before you say, 'What was the point of telling me then?' and throw the book at the wall, there is a very important piece of information I have to give you. When it comes to buying houses, you may well find it's the most important piece of factual experience in this book.

This crucial fact is:

It may appear that all doors are now firmly closed, double-locked and with a Welsh dresser wedged behind them when it comes to buying houses with little or no money down. These days, we are told that deals involving getting more than your initial outlay back are now firmly etched into 'credit crunch' history.

In reality, and contrary to what you may believe and the media portrays, you *can* still buy houses, with a net outlay of zero or better, that are capable of making you a good return.

Not only that, but the fantastic discounts I've achieved over the last few years are now considerably average by comparison to what you can get today, and what you may be able to get in the future. There are investors in my city (and yours) who are getting 30, 40 or even 50% off RIC's valuations on properties who are no smarter that you or I.

In history, many successful people have been so because they have either found something that worked and made it better (sometimes only fractionally) or, when everyone was turning to run away from the beast, they stopped, got a grip on their fear and faced it.

You may have guessed by now that I am a fan of the pugilists and, although I wouldn't dare to compare what I do to boxing, (which is much more strenuous) most people agree that a fighter can only *take* so many punches without the risk of long term damage or worse, and can only *make* so many punches before he or she becomes slow and ragged. Because of this they must train correctly and choose their peaks precisely and opponents well, as the pain they have to undergo in order to reach 'greatness' is non-sustainable indefinitely.

This brings me on to three final thoughts that I would like to leave with you.

Frank Bruno

Most people will have heard of the boxer, Frank Bruno. Throughout his career, he was known as a loveable giant with some humorous catch phrases and an infectious laugh.

Frank was never considered to be 'one of the greatest' and national campaigns were often run for him to retire after each of his losses.

Technically, he wasn't considered to 'float like a butterfly', was viewed by many to be slightly robotic, not the easiest of targets to miss and, arguably, didn't know when to take a count. Everyone in our family would watch his fights through our fingers when the big Americans started hitting him back.

Frank had one goal though, and that was to become heavyweight champion of the world, so he never gave up. Eventually, after several unsuccessful attempts, he achieved his dream. He proved that you don't have to be the best to get to the top; you just have to work on and around your weaknesses and maximise your strengths and at some point you will succeed. Among Frank's strengths were his huge courage, determination and quite possibly the hardest left jab in the business. Did his jab sting like a bee? Nope, more like a Scorpion tank! These, along with surrounding himself with good people, picking the right opponents and the correct knowledge of his sport, eventually took him to the top.

Pygmy Goats

The pygmy goat was originally from Africa. These mini-cousins to our native sheep and goats arrived in the United Kingdom somewhere around the end of the 19th Century and were kept as zoo animals. The pygmy goat is smaller than its dairy counterpart and, these days, is more likely to be kept as a pet. It may also produce a small amount of milk for its owner's consumption if required.

Now, a book about house shares may be the last place you'd expect to find a little bit of information about small goats, but I would like to tell you why this information may be very important to you.

There is now an almost certain probability that, if you were to ask the next fifty people you meet what they can tell you about pygmy goats, their knowledge on the subject would be inferior to yours. In fact, it is now likely that you are one of the most knowledgeable people on this subject within several miles of wherever you are now. If you were to spend an hour or so researching pygmy goats further then, very quickly, you could quite possibly become one of the most tangible sources of information on the subject in your town or city. Furthermore, if you were to meet some owners and breeders and researched their history and habitats, in a very short period of time you could become a world authority on the subject.

Now, unless you have found this information fascinating, I'm not saying that you should learn more about the pygmy goat. The point I am trying to make is that whatever you choose to do, learn it well. You will have the greatest chance of success in following your chosen path when you combine both passion and knowledge.

The Serene Beauty of the McDonalds Drive Through

If you're about the same age as me, you may now be pouting and saying, "What you talking 'bout Willis?" but if you live near a McDonalds Drive through, it will give you an invaluable lesson in business systems.

Before we even get to a McDonalds, if you have an Iphone or another smart phone, you can download an app which at the press of a button a will direct you to your nearest store from wherever you are in the country.

I'm not suggesting you eat the food, just order a coffee and look for clues as to what's happening during the whole process.

Firstly, you will drive along a little road around the store, past some very good advertising showing you the old favourites, along with items that you didn't even know McDonalds sell, such as fruit, milk and even porridge! You may not want these things right now, but this marketing 'system' has planted a very subtle seed in your brain that maybe it is not all burgers, fries and milkshakes.

When you get to window one, there is either someone waiting for you, or on their way to greet you. A system, quite often a pressure mat you drive over, has told the person working window one that you're coming. The window one person is never ever surprised to see you.

You are then asked what you would like, which is prompted by a system which is displaying a message on the till and your order is taken.

The system then decides on the most likely 'up sells' you may like and you are offered these along with sugar and a napkin.

The system then prompts them to tell you to have a great day and drive along to the next window.

Person 2 hasn't spoken to person 1, but I can see that they are by the coffee machine making my coffee. A system has sent them a message to go the coffee machine, pick up the right sized cup and press the button that will make my coffee. Their stock taking system ensures they never run out of cups or lids; the machines' systems lets the staff know when it needs more coffee beans, cleaning and it even knows the exact amount of beans to grind to make my coffee to eliminate as much waste and 'user error' as possible.

Window 2 is also in the right location, so that you can see what the staff are doing, so you know you're not being ignored as well as being in the correct proximity to the kitchen to ensure efficient foot flow by the staff.

Whichever McDonalds you go to, the coffee always tastes the same, as each restaurant follows the same operating systems and the machines, which are all programmed the same way, are making the coffee not the people.

With this in mind, McDonalds can grow as quickly as they like whilst employing a plentiful, low skilled labour force, whilst maintaining the same standards throughout the business. If everyone in a branch of McDonalds won the lottery and didn't turn in for work, that branch wouldn't fold; it wouldn't even be shut for days or weeks. Within a couple of hours, any McDonald's staff member from any branch could walk in, slot themselves into the 'McDonalds system' and the machine would march on.

McDonalds is probably the greatest example of being 'system dependant' over 'people dependant' thus creating a consistent service across its thousands of stores.

Everybody I know can build a better burger than McDonalds, but no one I know can build a better business!

The message I'm giving you here is that the more underlying systems you can incorporate into your house share business, the bigger you can grow and the easier it becomes.

From the moment a customer touches my company and until long after they have left me, 'systems' are working to draw them in, keep them happy and get them back if they leave.

If you're not doing this in your business, then it's time to start before your competitors do, or you'll burn out. You should always position yourself to be the 'control' and not the 'bottleneck' and it's never too late to start this.

If you need more help than this book can provide, visit www.housesharehero.co.uk for more information, tips and ideas on making house shares work brilliantly for you too!

If you're ready to be a House Share Hero, then train hard, learn your stuff, pick your battles well and manage your peaks.

If you want it, it's out there waiting for you.

And remember, if you are thinking, you are winning!

Until we meet
HouseShareHero.co.uk

Lightning Source UK Ltd.
Milton Keynes UK
01 February 2011

166744UK00001B/39/P

9 780956 050106